OCD Treatment Through Storytelling

OCD Treatment Through Storytelling

A Strategy for Successful Therapy

Allen H. Weg

OXFORD
UNIVERSITY PRESS
2011

OXFORD
UNIVERSITY PRESS

Oxford University Press, Inc., publishes works that further
Oxford University's objective of excellence
in research, scholarship, and education.

Oxford New York
Auckland Cape Town Dar es Salaam Hong Kong Karachi
Kuala Lumpur Madrid Melbourne Mexico City Nairobi
New Delhi Shanghai Taipei Toronto

With offices in
Argentina Austria Brazil Chile Czech Republic France Greece
Guatemala Hungary Italy Japan Poland Portugal Singapore
South Korea Switzerland Thailand Turkey Ukraine Vietnam

Published by Oxford University Press, Inc.
198 Madison Avenue, New York, New York 10016
www.oup.com

Library of Congress Cataloging-in-Publication Data
Weg, Allen Howard.

OCD treatment through storytelling : a strategy for successful therapy/Allen H. Weg.
p. ; cm.
Includes index.
ISBN 978-0-19-538356-0
1. Obsessive-compulsive disorder—Treatment. 2. Exposure therapy. I. Title.
[DNLM: 1. Obsessive-Compulsive Disorder—therapy. 2. Cognitive Therapy—methods.
3. Implosive Therapy—methods. 4. Narration. WM 176 W 411o 2011]
RC533.W442 2011
616.85'227—dc22 2010020138

1 3 5 7 9 8 6 4 2

Printed in the United States of America
on acid-free paper

To my mother, Sylvia Mauskopf Weg, a survivor of Auschwitz, who has courageously shared the most difficult stories there are to tell.

Acknowledgments

This book is the result of over two decades worth of learning about and working with obsessive compulsive disorder (OCD). The stories written herein developed naturally out of a need to better communicate to others the complex, confusing, and always changing world of OCD. But I needed to first learn about this world for myself before I could effectively teach it to others. For this, I need to thank the International OCD Foundation (IOCDF), until recently known as the Obsessive Compulsive Foundation. It was at this organization's annual conferences that I was first introduced to the leaders in the field of research and therapy for OCD and to the ever-growing number of texts and journal articles that continue to clarify our understanding of this disorder and offer ever-newer techniques and therapies to better treat it. Many of these professionals have become my respected colleagues, and I continue to learn and get inspiration from them. It was also at these conferences that I first encountered large numbers of people struggling with OCD: children there with their families, adolescents trying to manage an already difficult life stage encumbered unimaginably by this disorder, as well as adults who had suffered in silence and isolation for many years. It was at these conferences that I saw hopelessness turn to hopefulness, where I saw impotence turn into empowerment. It was there that I first experienced the warmth, love, pride, and strength that constitute the OCD community and that inspired me to make treating this disorder a large part of my life's work.

I would also like to thank the members of the Board of Directors of OCD NJ, an affiliate of the IOCDF, especially its president and treasurer, Ina and Julian Spero, who have dedicated the last 12 years of their postretirement lives to the support of the OCD community in the state of New Jersey and to the education of the general community about this disorder. I would also like to thank Board member Dr. Rachel Strohl, who functioned as my proofreader for this work.

Next, I wish to thank the publishers at Oxford University Press for their willingness to accept the proposal for this book, even though I was a relatively untested author and the content of the book was somewhat untraditional in its focus.

In addition, this book could not have been written were it not for the many clients and their families who have shared their struggles with OCD in their therapy sessions with me. It has been their willingness to "fly into the darkness" that has truly been the inspiration for the stories in this book. For a look inside the world of OCD, there have been no greater teachers.

Finally, I would like to thank my family for their love, support, and patience. My wife Nadine has had to share me all these years not only with my clients but with this particular labor of love. My children, Ethan and Arielle, now teenagers, hardly remember a time when I was not actively working on this book. Please know that I love you all and appreciate every sacrifice you have made.

Foreword

My father was a great storyteller. He never failed to have a story for any occasion or any audience, and I never tired of his stories. I could hear the same ones over and over again, and it was like hearing them for the first time. Not until later in my life did I realize that my father was not just entertaining when he told these stories. Through them, he not only made people laugh, he also made them feel comfortable, like insiders. Telling stories made people feel as though he understood what it was like to be in their shoes; his stories earned their trust. They could relate to him, and they felt he could relate to them. Most of all, the stories offered lessons about my father's values, his business principles, and his expectations of himself and others. As a result, they stuck with people. Even now, years after his death, people remember stories my father told them in a wide array of venues—business meetings, family gatherings, parties, funerals, and weddings. For them, my father's stories are clear and vivid, as if they just heard them yesterday. I fully believe this is one of the reasons people liked and trusted him so inherently.

I was reminded of my father and the power of his stories as I read *OCD Treatment Through Storytelling*. Allen Weg guides us through the therapeutic process of treating OCD in a truly unique way. By using stories to help clients and their families understand both the experience of the illness as well as the treatment process, Allen brings us a new approach to helping clients struggling with OCD.

I have known Allen for some years, both in my role as Program Director at the OCD Institute at McLean Hospital in Massachusetts and through my work as the President of the International OCD Foundation. Allen often refers clients to us at McLean, and I have come to know him as an extremely competent therapist who cares deeply about his clients. I also know that Allen spends countless hours volunteering for the New Jersey Affiliate of the OCD Foundation, supporting local efforts to assist people with OCD and their families by providing education and support. He is truly dedicated to this cause. He is the real deal.

Although the use of Exposure and Response Prevention (ERP) for OCD has been around for quite a while, and is well documented in the literature and in multiple books for both clinicians and lay people alike, it is clear that it is a difficult treatment to implement. Because it involves asking people to engage in activities that make them significantly anxious, things that they spend excessive amounts of time and energy trying not to do, it takes a special kind of person and a certain kind of relationship to achieve success. This is why the idea of introducing storytelling into the therapy is so compelling. By sharing stories, often from your own experiences, you are able to help people with OCD realize that they are not alone, how to persevere when things are difficult, and how to understand why it is important and necessary to feel so incredibly uncomfortable in order to get better. Most of all, the use of storytelling humanizes the experience and builds trust.

Facts are often an overused resource in an academic world. Explaining how or why ERP is successful using rating scales and percentage decreases in Yale-Brown Obsessive-Compulsive Scale (YBOCS) scores typically does not help people feel better about having to use a public bathroom if they are quite certain they are going to catch a deadly disease if they do. There are those people for whom explaining the treatment in simple terms, giving them assignments, and sending them on their way works just fine. If all people were like this, our jobs as treatment providers would be relatively simple! However, people are often more complicated than this, and using a one-pronged approach to treatment will often result in poor outcomes. Therefore, broadening our repertoire of resources for treating clients can only improve our chances of success.

Facts can also tend to be used against clients by family members who may be frustrated and angry about the impact of the OCD on their own lives. "Here is a treatment that works! Why won't you just do it?" Many of the stories that Allen uses in this book would be wonderful to share with families as a way of illustrating just how difficult it is to have OCD, as well as how challenging and scary the treatment is to do. By engendering this kind of empathy, the treatment enables families to be more supportive and less blaming throughout the treatment process, which also improves outcomes.

Perhaps most importantly of all, stories tend to stick when facts do not. Whereas I and others can remember in great detail the stories my father told us, and therefore the lessons they were meant to teach, there are all kinds of facts about the work I do every day that I have trouble remembering! Although helpful, facts are often uninspiring. It is more often the stories we hear illustrating those facts that we do remember and use to inspire us. The analogies and stories used by Allen in this book are easy to remember and can be called upon again and again, even when one is under periods of great stress. This may be their greatest strength.

I remember working with a young man many years ago at McLean. At that time my office was in a building at the top of a slight hill that was steeper at some parts than others. I remember one day in winter when the ground was frozen and slippery, watching this patient attempting to climb up the steeper part of the hill to return to the building. He kept slipping and sliding back down the hill, over and over again. He would get back up and try again in the exact same way to climb up the hill. Never did it seem to occur to him to try walking around to a flatter section or to side-step up the hill. He just kept going at it head on—and falling back. This is often what happens with therapists who take a singular approach to their therapy. Although such an approach may work for some clients, others are going to be like this patient, who, for whatever reason, cannot make good use of this one approach and so will never make any progress. As treatment providers, it is up to us to help our clients find alternatives. This book provides us with a terrific roadmap.

I often wish that I could tell stories as well as my father did. It seemed to me no accident that my younger brother, who is the most like my father, became a documentary filmmaker, and tells stories for a living now. Allen's book has made me wonder, however, whether we can all be good storytellers. Surely our everyday experiences can help our clients in some way to understand and engage in a difficult treatment more fully. Until I get better at it, I plan to use this book as my guide. I encourage you to do the same.

Diane Davey, RN, MBA
Program Director
OCD Institute
McLean Hospital
Belmont, MA

Contents

OCD Treatment Through Storytelling

Introduction

Many books have been written about obsessive-compulsive disorder (OCD). Some are specifically for professionals, with instructions on diagnosis and treatment. Others are geared toward those persons struggling with OCD themselves and often include first-hand testimonials, words of encouragement, listings of resources, and information about self-help techniques. Still others address the concerns of family members, especially parents, and give direction and advice on how to cope with and respond to a loved one with OCD. For the most part, these books provide a great service. They are instructive and informative and help those whose lives are in some way touched by this mental disorder.

OCD Treatment Through Storytelling is my attempt to offer something different. Although I have geared the book toward clinicians, I have made sure to write it in such a way that lay people will understand it, so those with OCD and their friends and family members may also find this book helpful in their efforts to understand for themselves and explain to others just what it feels like to have OCD.

This book is also different because it reveals the intimate, internal experience of a person who has OCD in a way that I believe has not previously been the focus in an OCD text. In addition, I present a rationale for the cognitive-behavioral treatment of the disorder, which often may appear more strange and bizarre than the disorder itself—especially to those experiencing it for the first time. I address situations in which treatment can fail and show how therapists can help their clients to regain the upper hand when it does. I explain in no uncertain terms the struggle between the mental illness known as obsessive-compulsive disorder and the people who challenge it: be they those who treat it, those who have it, or those who love someone who has it. What makes my book unique is that I do all of this completely *through the use of storytelling and metaphor.*

The use of storytelling and metaphor—what does that mean, exactly? Storytelling and metaphor use are often the best ways to present subtle and confusing ideas in a succinct and concrete way. In fact, they are wonderful ways to go beyond merely describing something or even explaining it. Narratives serve to illustrate not just an idea, but the very foundation of an idea. By hearing a story, the listener shares an experience with the narrator that enables him to understand what is being discussed in a way that mere description cannot accomplish. In a way, the listener is able to get inside the mind of the narrator.

Narratives serve to illustrate not just an idea, but the very foundation of an idea.

Obsessive-compulsive disorder is relatively simple and easy to describe in clinical terms, but it is extremely difficult to fully understand. Once presented with information about this psychiatric disorder, many are left with the questions, "Okay, I get what happens, but how can that be?" "How does that make sense?" "Why are people thinking and doing those crazy things?"

"How can a person who seems completely normal and competent in so many areas of his or her life waste so much time engaged in the most ridiculous, nonsensical behaviors?" "How can it be possible that someone who is a successful marriage partner, parent, professional, or all three, is unable to touch something that everyone else has no problem touching?" "Why would someone with a higher than average IQ find the need to read the same passage in a book over and over again?"

"How can it be that someone who never acted out aggressively, and has a good relationship with her mother, finds that she dare not go into the kitchen because there are knives there, and she fears that she might impulsively grab a knife and attack her mother?" "How can someone who can quickly and decisively research and purchase a car or big-screen TV spend hours struggling with the question of which pair of socks is the one that is 'just right' to wear that day?" "What about someone who professes to be an atheist finding that whenever he hears any form of the word 'death' he has to repeat the equivalent form of the word 'life' five times in order to feel 'safe'?"

People with apparently excellent and sound judgment, people who are responsible, decisive, and spontaneous in most aspects of their lives, will often become completely unable to demonstrate these qualities and strengths when faced with the most mundane of tasks and activities. Chances are you have already encountered people like these in your clinical practice. The purpose of this book is to help promote improved communication and empathy with your OCD clients and thereby support the therapeutic process.

The contradictions of OCD are what first drew me into working with this disorder. People diagnosed with OCD can be completely lucid but can appear completely psychotic. Their thought processes about the rituals that they need to perform sound outrageously foreign to most people yet at the same time, somehow hauntingly familiar. Rarely do I tell someone what specialty area I practice in without a resulting comment about an in-law or sibling who could use my services. Yet, as strange as OCD symptoms are, they do not hold a candle to its most empirically tested and effective treatment. The cognitive-behavioral treatment of OCD, exposure and response prevention (ERP), involves some of the most bizarre and outrageous interventions that you are ever likely to conduct in a therapy office. Most OCD clients are very surprised or even stunned when I explain to them what they need to do in order to help make themselves better. They sometimes think their therapist is crazier than they feel.

And so something beyond telling is required. Explanations seem insufficient when one is being instructed to think and behave in a way that seems contradictory to one's goals—or in a way that is at times profoundly uncomfortable, even painful. This is what ERP treatment for OCD asks clients to do.

As I worked with OCD clients over the years, I found that the most effective way for me to share my perspective on their struggles, and to introduce them to the unexpected treatment strategies required for control of the disorder, was not to talk to them about OCD at all. Instead, I found myself talking about completely unrelated things, such as events from my personal life or shared experiences from the mass media and the like, in order to make a certain point or to get at the concept behind an OCD symptom or a treatment intervention.

This idea is not a new one. Philosophers and religious leaders have used storytelling as a form of instruction since the beginning of civilization. The stories in the Hebrew Bible are understood by some not as a historical review of events that actually took place but rather as a provision of moral, ethical, and religious instruction through the use of storytelling. The New Testament likewise is full of parables that require interpretation in order to best understand the message being delivered. In the arts, whether we are referring to dance, music, sculpture, painting, writing, poetry, theatre, or film making, there are countless examples of an emotion, a struggle, or an experience of some kind that is communicated indirectly and expressed through the artistic medium. These artistic representations, when done effectively, allow the audience to better understand what is being communicated than if the ideas were being presented through mere instruction.

As I found myself better understanding the nuances of the different OCD symptom presentations, becoming more experienced in prescribing more and more creative interventions, and witnessing different variations in the struggle between clients and the mental illness that had gripped them, I also found myself increasingly relying on the use of storytelling. I would search for the words to better get across an idea to a client or family member, only to suddenly hear myself sharing a story or a personal anecdote to illustrate a feeling, a strategy, a dynamic, or an intervention. Metaphor was my way of communicating, "I really *get* what you are going through," in a way that nothing else could. In addition, it was a way to help frustrated and frightened family members understand the phenomenological experience of the person in their lives who had OCD. Storytelling was also a way to explain to clients and their loved ones that the therapy, which at first glance could easily be rejected as nonsense, was indeed the most powerful set of tools available for them to get their lives back. Finally, I found it to be a wonderful and entertaining way to educate and train other mental health professionals about the symptom presentation and treatment interventions for this disorder. That is why I have written this book.

I would search for the words to better get across an idea to a client or family member, only to suddenly hear myself sharing a story or a personal anecdote to illustrate a feeling, a strategy, a dynamic, or an intervention.

I am not the first person to do this. I have rarely been to a presentation on the topic of OCD without the speaker utilizing some form of storytelling to illustrate a particular aspect of this topic. Likewise, many of the books that I have read on OCD will on occasion employ non-OCD stories to make certain points. However, never before has there been a book about OCD that uses storytelling as the focus of its content, as a way of promoting and reinforcing treatment.

OCD Treatment Through Storytelling relies on storytelling and the use of metaphors almost exclusively as the method of instruction. Over the years, I began to record the stories I was using in my therapy sessions, preserving them for future use with other clients. Eventually I found I had amassed quite an anthology. This book is the result of that collection of recorded anecdotes, stories, and metaphors. I believe that these are all original, but it is possible that I have unwittingly adopted a story or anecdote here that I first read or heard elsewhere. If so, I apologize to the original author and, if I am made aware of the original source, will freely and willingly give credit where it is due. Now I am sharing these stories with you, telling them in exactly the same way as I would in a therapy session to a client and/or his or her family, or in the way I would review them in a presentation to a group of fellow professionals learning how to treat this disorder. I hope that they will at once inform, educate, and entertain.

A few brief notes of clarification. First, this book reviews not so much a new or different methodology for the treatment of OCD but, rather, a specific "delivery system" designed for a more effective implementation of already established clinical practices. If you are a clinician already experienced in the application of these clinical interventions in your practice, I hope that you find that this text provides a fresh look at the way in which you can introduce these interventions to your clients. On the other hand, whether professional or layperson, if you are not already familiar with these practices, or are only generally familiar with them, this text is a great way to get introduced to them or deepen your understanding of them.

A second item that I would like to bring to your attention is that although the majority of clinical interventions outlined in this book have been carefully studied and reviewed in the literature, this is not the case when it comes to the use of storytelling as it relates to the treatment of OCD. The cognitive-behavioral treatment of OCD is an evidenced-based approach and has met the rigorous tests of researchers, who have written and published extensively about these interventions in clinical journals and books of various kinds. In contrast, telling stories in therapy as a way of teaching about these techniques and as a way of addressing multiple issues in OCD treatment has not been subjected to the same kinds of rigorous tests. "Pure" cognitive-behavioral therapists, and especially those who are primarily researchers, might suggest that the use of storytelling has not been clearly demonstrated to improve client recovery in OCD treatment. They would be correct in this assertion.

Still, I have found through personal clinical experience over many years, and through casual conversation with many other respected clinicians who are "OCD specialists," that utilizing storytelling in treatment can enhance progress and recovery. I will leave it to the researchers to show that in fact formal study of this process supports its use. For now, you only have my personal observations as a clinician to go by.

How this Book Is Organized

The book is essentially a list of the stories that I have written and used in treatment over the years; however, they do not stand entirely alone. For all the stories that are presented, during some part of the storytelling, almost always at the very end, there is a corresponding section titled "The OCD Connection." In this section are a few words, sentences, or paragraphs that connect the story to some aspect of the OCD experience. In this way the book is not *just* a listing of narratives, one after the other. Instead, the points that are being made within the story, whether it is specific information about the phenomenological experience of having the disorder, specific instruction on how to employ cognitive-behavioral treatment strategies to the disorder, an empathic sharing of emotional experiences such as fear or frustration, or the communication of motivation through encouragement, hope, or empowerment, are then reviewed within the context of OCD. Therefore, for each story, after the narrative ends I make some comments directly to you, the reader, regarding the point of the story and its relevance to the OCD experience.

The stories are organized by chapters, with each chapter addressing some common aspect of OCD or its treatment. I recommend that the chapters be read in the order in which they are presented, but feel free to skip around, as if it were a reference text, reading only those stories that are of interest to you or that are pertinent to a particular clinical challenge. The only exceptions to this are the first three stories in chapter 2, which should be read in succession. A list of all the stories appears at the back of this book for easy reference.

Chapter 1 introduces the basics. What are obsessions and compulsions? What does it feel like to have OCD, and what are the different ways that it may be manifested? Although many of the stories in this book are inventions to illustrate a point, you will see immediately that I often draw on my own experiences to help communicate an OCD-related concept. Even though these latter-type stories are of a more personal nature, I believe that the experiences they describe are usually universal and that most people will be able to relate to them. Chapter 2 introduces us to the bedrock of the cognitive-behavioral treatment of OCD, exposure and response prevention (ERP), or simply, exposure therapy. Chapter 3 details the behavioral aspects of ERP, and chapter 4 looks at the cognitive considerations of this treatment. Chapter 5 addresses concerns that people have when their OCD symptoms persist even after treatment with this therapy.

Some stories that specifically address OCD in the child are offered in chapter 6, and chapter 7 provides stories that illustrate how the concept of trust is an important component in the successful application of OCD treatment interventions. The stories presented in chapter 8 illustrate cognitive tools to help clients cope with relapse and the waxing and waning nature of OCD. Finally, in chapter 9, some special topics of interest are covered. These include dealing with resistance to treatment, the problems associated with hoarding as well as health-focused OCD, and ways in which family members may be affected by the disorder.

Certain themes, even specific phrases or very detailed concepts, will reappear in several stories. This is not an accident. Although I believe it is important to communicate certain ideas to clients with OCD, I have found that people may react very differently to similar stories that embed the same lessons. For whatever reason, a client or colleague may respond favorably to a particular story that I have shared and therefore internalize the concept that story conveyed. These same people, however, may not feel the same way about another story that has at its center the very same idea. I therefore tend to tell some stories that overlap in the messages that they communicate and expect that some will resonate better with some people, whereas other stories will resonate better with other people. I have included several of these "overlapping stories" in the present collection of narratives.

As you move through the therapeutic process of teaching and employing ERP with your clients, you can use this book as a resource to help address many of the issues that arise as you encounter different aspects of treatment. For example, when you are sharing with your clients the rationale for employing ERP, you might simply say to them,

"Let me share with you a story that I think might help you understand this better," and then tell one of the stories or metaphors designed to illustrate the concept of exposure therapy. Likewise, when you are supporting them as they express their doubts about being able to face their fears as they move forward in treatment, you can introduce one of the stories designed to help clients to think differently about their relationship to fear. Also, when you are helping them to deal with their frustration if they seem to lose ground in the course of treatment, you might say, "I know it is hard to not feel discouraged when you seem to be going backwards after so much hard work, but perhaps I can help you get refocused and reenergized with a story demonstrating how progress can often get derailed, yet continue to move forward toward success ..." This book can be used in a like manner for many of the issues and struggles that are part of being in therapy, introducing stories or metaphors as a natural part of the discussion during the course of a session.

Keep in mind, however, that *OCD Treatment Through Storytelling* is not so much a text on information as it is a text on education. What do I mean by this? First, it is not comprehensive or all inclusive. For instance, medication, which is considered by most professionals to be an important part of treatment for a great number of OCD cases, is not addressed in these stories. Second, this book is less about facts and more about having a feeling, an understanding, of the world of OCD. Finally, well-told stories, whether they are about one's personal family history, one's people, culture, religion, or country, or stories about humankind in general, demand to be repeated. "Daddy, tell us again about how you and Mommy met!" is the kind of refrain heard in many a household. Most parents are surprised at how their children never seem to tire of hearing the same bedtime stories over and over, night after night. And how many of us watch the same movie again and again to recapture some part of the experience, even though once we have seen it, we already know how it ends? I therefore suggest that you encourage your clients to think repeatedly about these stories. You should also consider referencing stories repeatedly over the course of therapy as appropriate to whatever issues are being discussed. In addition, feel free to use these stories as a starting point in developing your own anthology of metaphors and anecdotes. Soon you will have a

This book is less about facts and more about having a feeling, an understanding, of the world of OCD.

rich collection of stories to use over and over in your own clinical practice. Share them with those who you think will benefit from what they have to say. My hope is that you will find, as I have, that stories can provide for you and for your clients an unparalleled sense of empowerment and be a source of support, validation, and hope.

1

Obsessions and Compulsions

The stories in this chapter provide a general overview of OCD. I use metaphors to describe and define obsessions and compulsions and to illustrate the role of doubting in many individuals' experiences of OCD. I then go on to explain how OCD can manifest differently for different people.

Student Driver

When I was 17 years old, I took a driver's education course, as did most of my contemporaries back in Queens, New York. Four eager high school students would cram into a sedan with a very nervous instructor sitting in the front passenger seat. We could not wait to master the skill that would catapult us into the kind of independence and freedom that eluded younger adolescents. After several lessons spent driving around the parking lot and later up and down small streets, we finally got our chance to take the car out onto the highway. And so it was announced that we would be driving on the Grand Central Parkway that day—a major highway in the area. We were thrilled when the day arrived, but also quite nervous.

We were to take turns at the steering wheel, and I was the first to go. There I was, driving on the highway! The instructor was sitting in the passenger seat beside me, and the three other students were in the back. I was driving along in the slow lane, and after a few moments, the instructor told me to move into the middle lane. Then, in just another moment, to my simultaneous delight and horror, he instructed me to get into the passing, or "hammer," lane. My memory of driving those first few moments in the hammer lane is incredibly clear, as is the case with most memories of life experiences that have elicited extremely powerful emotional responses.

I was traveling at about 55, maybe 60 miles per hour, and my hands, located at the standard 10 o'clock and 2 o'clock positions on the steering wheel, were clenched so tightly that my knuckles were beginning to turn white. And then the strangest thing happened. I remember thinking to myself, just for an instant, "You know, I could just turn this steering wheel eight or ten inches to the left or right, and instantaneously a whole bunch of people would get killed!" This was a very strange thought indeed, and I remember at the time wondering where in the world such a thought could have come from. In retrospect, however, it is clear to me that up until that point in my life, I had never been in a situation where I had that kind of power—where one small body movement would result in that kind of an instant devastation. And so the occasion to have such a thought had never arisen before.

I thought about the possibility of purposely crashing the car for all of about 30 seconds. I visualized it in my mind's eye and could even hear the brief screams quickly interrupted by the sounds of screeching tires and of metal crashing against metal. I got a brief burst of anxiety followed by a shiver down my spine, and a moment later it was all over. The thought was gone, and the fear with it. "Well that's just stupid," I remember thinking to myself. "I would just never do that." And that was that.

The OCD Connection

What I had experienced that day, a long time ago on the Grand Central Parkway, was in effect, an obsession. The only difference between what happened to me in that car and what happens to people with OCD is that *they* cannot "just forget about it." It sticks. It gets played over and over again in their heads. They cannot let go of it. The ability of my brain to distance from the thought, to trust that even though I was fully capable of turning that steering wheel, I would not, is something that the person with OCD has difficulty doing. We all get strange and nonsensical obsessions at times. This experience is not limited to those with the diagnosis of OCD. Those of us, however, who are without the disorder are usually able to accept them as mere thoughts and to recognize

We all get strange and nonsensical obsessions at times.

that we need not attend to them seriously. Those afflicted with OCD cannot easily do this.

Locked Out

When I was in graduate school, it was often the case that several class assignments were all due at around the same time. There were also many occasions when I had to sit for several exams within a few days, sometimes even a few hours, of each other. During those times I found myself experiencing extreme levels of stress.

In the field of stress management, we have found that people differ from each other not only in the particular things that they find stressful but also in their own personal response to stress, which is termed the person's "stress response pattern." Some people cannot sleep, while others sleep too much; some stop eating, while others tend to overeat; some develop headaches, while others develop digestive difficulties. One of the signs that I am under great stress, one of my personal stress response patterns, has always been to forget and mislay things. So, if I'm in my office and I'm on my fourth or fifth pen because I keep misplacing them, I know that it has been a stressful day.

While I was in graduate school, there was one particular week when I had three tests and two term papers due. During that same week, I locked myself out of my car ... *twice*. This was a time before car remotes were ubiquitous, and in order to lock your car, you would need to push the button down on the inside of your car door, then step out of the car and slam the door shut while holding the outside door handle in an "up" position. Well, my stress response pattern was in full swing that week, and I employed the locking door technique described above, but left the keys inside the car while doing it. I actually did it twice within three days, each time leaving the keys inside the car. I had to phone the police each time to get them out. They were able to do this quite expediently, by the way, and I remember feeling a little unnerved at how easy it was for them to break into my car with just a flat piece of tin.

In any event, as a result of leaving the keys in the car the way that I did, I developed, without purposely meaning to, an interesting habit. Whenever I parked the car, I would engage in the following set of behaviors: I would put the car in park, take the keys out of the ignition, and get out of the car with keys in hand. I would then stand outside the car with the car door still open, and I would hold the door handle in the "up" position with my left hand, ready to shut the door and lock it. At the same time I would be holding the car keys in my right hand. While standing there, I would pull my right hand up where I could see it, squeeze the keys in that hand for about three seconds, and say out loud in an audible voice the word "keys." It was only after completing this set of behaviors in just the way that I have described them here that I felt comfortable enough to shut the door, locking it.

The OCD Connection

My behavior with my keys was a ritual, or a compulsion—clearly as much a compulsion as any other OCD ritual out there. And although, given my experience of having locked myself out of the car, the behavior seems no more than perhaps an exaggerated act of being careful, most people do not go around squeezing their car keys and talking out loud to themselves as they shut the car door.

But there *are* some important differences between my behavior and that of someone with OCD. The differences are that it took me only three seconds a few times a day at most; it did not interfere with my functioning in any way, and it did not create any additional stress for me. My key ritual was just this thing that I did. If someone challenged me to forgo the checking behavior on any occasion, I probably would have been able to do so with only moderate discomfort. Yet it still *was* a ritual, a compulsion, in the sense that it *did* feel uncomfortable for me *not* to do it and that I felt comfortable shutting that car door only *after* I did the ritual. OCD compulsions, however, are defined as behaviors or behavioral sets that significantly interfere with or limit a person's functioning in some way. Because this set of behaviors did not in any way interfere with my level of functioning—an extra three seconds to get out the car was hardly disruptive—it would not qualify as a compulsion as we define it in OCD.

Having rituals or compulsions, just as was the case with obsessions, is the stuff of life. We all experience them both quite regularly, without much concern or thought. They are those fleeting thoughts and mental images that, more often than not, we quite easily dismiss, or those quirky habits that we just chalk up to being one of our personal eccentricities.

Having rituals or compulsions, just as was the case with obsessions, is the stuff of life.

But what if we got stuck in one of those thoughts and could not just dismiss it? What if that quirky habit took on a life of its own, taking up more and more of our time, becoming more complicated and convoluted until it really started to get in the way of our lives rather than helping us to cope with it? This is the world of those with OCD. They have no behaviors or thoughts uniquely their own. We have all experienced weird and strange thoughts and have all engaged in ridiculous, nonsensical, superstitious, and purposeless behaviors. What distinguishes those with OCD from the rest of us is nothing more than their inability to move beyond where they are at.

Crisis in the Oval Office

John lives in the Washington, DC area and works in a factory that manufactures electronic components. He works on an assembly line and has a very simple, very repetitive, very boring job. All day long John assembles the electrical connections in a particular piece of equipment.

There are four wires: red, blue, orange, and green. All John has to do when the product moves down to him on the production line is to take the red wire and the blue wire and twist the exposed ends together, creating a connection. He then takes the orange and the green wires and twists *them* together, completing a second circuit. This he does all day long, hour after hour.

Over the course of the day, John will often go into a hypnotic state. This is something that happens to most of us when we are engaged in repetitive actions and is most commonly experienced when driving a car on a familiar route, such as one would do when commuting the same way to work every day. In that context, we call this phenomenon "highway hypnosis." In general, if we are doing something really repetitive, we are probably in a state of highway hypnosis much of the time. This is in fact exactly what would happen to John. If you went to John at the end of the day and you said, "Do you think you got all the orange and green wires together and all the red and blue ones together in the right way?" He would most likely say, "Yeah probably, no problem. I'm fine." John is fairly certain that he did not make any mistakes on the assembly line that day. He has come to trust that while he is not always fully aware of what he is doing because of the highway hypnosis effect, he is doing his job well. Furthermore, he is so used to the repetitive action of connecting his colored wires that if something out of the ordinary had occurred that day, he is very confident that he would have noticed and dealt with the problem appropriately. In fact, John has developed a reputation in the DC area as being an extremely competent worker. He knows his colors, and he knows his wires.

John's brother-in-law works at the White House, and on this particular day, a terrible event has occurred. Terrorists have somehow gotten a fully armed nuclear warhead into the Oval Office. Bomb squads have been called in, and they have determined that the warhead is too dangerous to move and must be disarmed right there in the White House. After much deliberation, they figure out that there is only one way to disarm the warhead. There are four loose wires: blue, red, green, and orange. What is required is for the blue and red wires to be connected, and for the green and orange ones to be connected. Then all that needs to be done is for a switch on the side of the warhead to be turned off, and the bomb will be disarmed. If, however, the wrong wires are connected to each other, the bomb will detonate instantly when the switch is turned off.

John's brother-in-law, who is intimately aware of John's area of expertise, notifies the White House staff, and they immediately send for him. The bomb squad explains the details of the situation to John and then say to him, "What you have to do for us is twist together the blue with the red wire, and the green with the orange wire, just like you do a thousand times a day. Then we just flip the switch to deactivate the warhead. Of course, if you don't do it correctly and we flip the switch, then half the East Coast is going to be blown away." So there is a little bit of pressure here on John.

John stands in the Oval Office leaning over the front of the warhead, examining the situation. He takes a deep breath, and carefully twists the wires together the way he does a thousand times a day, every single day, week after week, month after month, year after year. He then stares for a bit at the wires.

Members of the bomb squad, who are crouched behind a couch on the other side of the room (as if that could protect them should the warhead detonate) hear John say out loud to himself, "Okay, the orange is connected to the green and the red is connected to the blue. I see it.

It is there. Right. It's definitely there." He touches the wires with his hands to make sure they are connected in the correct way. "There. I'm looking at it. I'm holding it. It looks right… but what if…"

"What's going on? Have you connected the wires correctly?" cries the bomb squad leader from across the room.

"I'm still not sure!" is the reply.

"Whadya *mean* you're 'still not sure?!' Did you connect them or didn't you?"

"Well, I connected them," comes the reply.

"So? Can we flip the switch?"

"Wait… I'm still not completely sure…"

Now, how can John be so unsure of something he watched himself do? He held those wires in his own hands, he studied them with his own eyes, he even reassuringly reviewed verbally that the task was done. How can he still question himself, especially *John*—the most expert blue-to-red/green-to-orange wire connector in the country? After all, this is the same guy who, even when not paying attention because of the phenomenon of highway hypnosis, feels very confident that he has successfully connected those wires. What is different?

The difference, of course, is that the consequences of being wrong are so much greater here. If John makes an error on the assembly line, the component will not work and the electronic device will malfunction. The result is that the electronic device holding the component will need to be returned. In the Oval Office, an error means the end to John's life and many other lives. It means instant death to millions of people in the Northeastern United States, and the complete destruction of the center of leadership of the free world on this planet.

The OCD Connection

This is what underlies the doubting experience of those with OCD. They are like John in the Oval Office. The only difference between John and somebody who has OCD is that John is very clear about what the consequences of his error would be. The person who has OCD feels anxiety as a result of what he believes "might happen."

The person who has OCD feels anxiety as a result of what he believes "might happen."

For instance, for a person suffering with a contamination/washing form of OCD thoughts such as, "I might get sick and die," or "I might make someone else get sick and die," are common attributions to the anxiety of not washing one's hands.

By believing that the potential consequences of not washing one's hands are extreme and severe (for example, "people might die,") the person with OCD elevates the act of washing one's hands to the importance level of John working with the wires in the Oval Office rather than working on the assembly line (which is how most of us feel about washing our hands). The consequences of *not* washing become so great that the level of self-doubt is increased.

The feeling that a person has while performing the ritual, the intensity of his anxiety stemming from the thought, "what happens if I get it wrong?" is no different from the way John felt when he was working in the Oval Office and waiting for the guy to flip that switch. Because of that, the doubting, just as in the case of John, escalates. Washers can examine their own hands even while they are washing, see with their very own eyes that their hands are clean, and still doubt it. They turn assembly-line situations into Oval Office situations, escalating doubt and fueling anxiety, resulting in the need to repeat, lengthen, or slow down the compulsive action.

This is torture for people with OCD. When signing a check to pay a bill, for instance, and getting ready to put it in the envelope to be mailed, they can look at the check, study it, touch it, hold it, and check again. Even while it is in their hands, as they are examining it, they are not sure. What if they accidentally made the check out for $1000 instead of $100? Or forgot to sign it? They do not trust their own senses. They feel what John felt in the Oval Office. When the OCD gets really bad, that is what it is like for people with OCD.

Casual observers, even if they understand the need to wash or check or ritualize in some other way, often have problems with the repetitiveness of the behavior. They often say things like, "Okay, I get it, you have to do this thing, but enough already! Why can't you just sort of let go of it, just forget it, just move on?" People with OCD would say, "Well, if I could do that, I would!" But this still leaves the observer in the dark. The concept of getting caught in the ritual can be hard to grasp. Sharing the concept of "Oval Office" thinking may help therapists to better communicate empathy with their clients, and better explain to family members the phenomenological experience of the disorder.

Allergies

Some people have multiple allergies to different foods. They report they have struggled with this condition since they were little kids.

They complain about memories of the heartache of watching their friends eating peanut butter sandwiches or strawberries without a thought while they were deprived of such treats because of their allergic sensitivity. Others complain about their need to be cautious about a variety of foods because of a single, often hidden, ingredient such as peanuts or wheat gluten.

However, despite the inconvenience of these allergic problems, these sufferers have for the most part been able to spare themselves the physical discomfort or at times even the life-threatening anaphylactic shock that may result from these allergic reactions. This can be accomplished through tedious self-education about the content of the foods around them, hypervigilance about what they eat, and the careful exercise of self-discipline.

But this is not true for all allergy sufferers. Seasonal allergies, unlike specific allergies such as food allergies or animal dander allergies, cannot be so easily controlled via avoidance. Although medication can be particularly helpful to many, some people cannot tolerate the side effects or do not experience the same level of relief from the use of medication as do most others. For these people, coping with allergies can be a very challenging task. Even regular air conditioning may not provide the necessary protection from environmental allergens, and special filtering machines may be required. Their allergic state is not a specific reaction to a specific activity, such as eating a forbidden food or going to a pet owner's home, but rather, it is omnipresent for certain times of the year and in certain parts of the country, torturing the sufferer for weeks or months at a time with little recourse for control or relief.

The OCD Connection

This depiction of two different types of allergy sufferers has a corollary in the world of OCD. On the one hand, the OCD sufferer may experience his OCD as a specific stimulus reaction in response to a very specific environmental trigger, in the same way that some people will have an allergic reaction only when they eat certain foods.

In OCD, this is most clear with those people who are motor vehicle accident checkers, or "MVA" checkers. For some of these people, their obsessions are triggered only when they drive, and they get flooded with thoughts that they have hit someone and might get into trouble for having fled the site of an accident. Their attempts to neutralize these fears are usually limited to driving back repeatedly over the same route to check for bodies, ambulances, or police activity or searching through newspapers or TV news channels in an attempt to see if any hit-and-run accidents have been reported. Although a particular obsession may plague them for long periods of time, even years, the *source* of a particular obsession is a specific incident—a particular ride by a school that was letting children out, for instance, or a rainy drive past a bicyclist. For these people with OCD, as much as they are vulnerable to the emotional pain of the disorder, through avoidance of driving they can exact some control over their OCD experience and avoid the obsessive-compulsive cycle.

Likewise, in the case of a typical contamination phobia, the OCD sufferer experiences heightened anxiety only if he is exposed to a perceived contaminant. Although neutralization is achieved through ritualistic washing, avoidance of potentially contaminated places or situations can minimize the experience of the OC struggle.

In these ways, the checker and the washer are much like those with food allergies. They are terribly inconvenient, but one can successfully influence the degree to which one's reactions are triggered in the first place, thus minimizing suffering by changing life habits and adjusting to the restrictions that the disorder generates. (Not to suggest that this is the most prudent of choices, as you negatively impact the quality of your life, but you could, at least temporarily, minimize anxiety.)

On the other hand, there are people with OCD whose suffering more closely resembles that of the seasonal allergy sufferer. These are people who do not present with any one set of OCD triggers but rather a multitude of triggers, which wax, wane, overlap, and morph constantly. Their experience of doubt and danger is not limited to a specific set of circumstances but rather is triggered by the process of living itself. These are the people who feel they must engage in rituals to get out of bed, to wash and dress, to eat breakfast, and to walk the dog. They are most often in a constant state of self-doubt and anxiety and can successfully avoid this anxiety only if they stop doing virtually everything. Even then they are not fully free of the constant obsessive state.

These latter OC sufferers are particularly vulnerable to depression because they are so overwhelmed by the complexity of their experience. Not to minimize the suffering of those with simpler forms of OCD, those with nonspecific OCD get even less respite and relief from their constant obsessive state, just as the seasonal allergy sufferer has no recourse but to move to another region of the country or wait for the seasons to change.

Yet the treatment for this nonspecific OCD remains the same as that for the more specific type. This includes acceptance of the state of doubt—even the purposeful exacerbation of it—labeling it as an OCD symptom, "avoidance of avoidance" whenever possible, and remembering that by "surrendering" the idea of combating these thoughts directly, the sufferer can ultimately transcend even those obsessions that remain active and lead normal, productive lives.

For therapists, being able to relate to stories like these allows for a better ability not only to naturally empathize with the anxiety experienced by their clients but also to express a deeper understanding of the very dynamics generating that anxiety. By sharing these stories with clients and their significant others, you demonstrate the depth of your knowledge of the internal experience of people who struggle with OCD, engendering greater trust in your ability to assist them. This is essential, as you will be relying on this trust as you guide them toward the very difficult treatment that lies ahead.

By sharing these stories with clients and their significant others, you demonstrate the depth of your knowledge of the internal experience of people who struggle with OCD.

2

Exposure and Response Prevention Therapy

The stories in this chapter provide an introduction to exposure therapy. Many clients with OCD are confused and fearful of exposure exercises, as they often seem counterintuitive and difficult to execute. The stories presented here explain the purpose and benefit of exposure exercises.

The Bee Trap

A bee trap is a device that people install in their backyards. It attracts, traps, and kills bees, keeping them away from you and your guests when you are having a picnic or barbeque. Most people can make the device themselves. It's simple—here's how.

Take a two- or three-liter, clear-colored soda bottle (not one that is tinted), empty the soda out of it, and tear off the label. Next, pour a little honey into the bottle and let it dry at the bottom. Turn the bottle upside down and tape a large paper clip or picture wire bent into a U shape to what is now the top of the bottle. This allows you to hang your bee trap bottle upside down from a tree limb or fence post. But before the trap can work, you have to do one more thing.

Take some black electrical tape and, starting about two-thirds of the way down from what is now the top of the bottle, wrap it around the circumference of the bottle progressing downward toward the spout. Continue to wrap it around itself past the opening of the bottle and then cut it, leaving only a very small opening for the bees to enter. Now it is ready to be hung.

When a bee enters the yard, it can detect the honey (it doesn't really smell it as we do, but it knows where the honey is), and it will fly to the bottle instead of bothering you and your friends. It enters into the tiny little hole at the bottom where you snipped off the electrical tape and flies up inside the bottle to the top where it finds the dried honey.

It extracts what it needs from the honey, and then it's time to leave the bottle. Now, bees are programmed so that when they are in an enclosure of some kind, like a cave or the hollow of a tree trunk, they instinctively know that the way out is in the direction of the light. So the bee essentially says to itself, "Well, I'll go where the light is, that's the way out." It attempts to fly toward the light, but of course the clear plastic wall of the bottle is in the way. Bees don't know about plastic, so the bee keeps hurling its body against the side of the bottle in an effort to escape, over and over again, until it finally dies right there in the bottle.

Why does it do that? After several attempts, why doesn't it just say to itself, "Duh! I'll just fly out the way I flew in, by going out the little hole in the bottom of the bottle!" Why? Because we *darkened* the bottom part of the bottle when we put the black tape around it. Therefore, whenever the bee heads toward the bottom of the bottle, it heads into the darker part of the enclosure. To the bee, it feels like it is going in the *wrong* direction. So it flies back up to the top, which keeps it stuck in the enclosure.

The truth is the only way out of the bottle is to fly into the darkness. It doesn't make sense to the bee because usually the way out of something is to fly toward the light. It's counterintuitive to go toward the darkness; it feels to the bee as though it is going deeper into the bottle rather than escaping. But in this case, flying toward the darkness, going in what feels like the wrong direction, is the only way out of the trap.

The OCD Connection

And that is what OCD treatment is like. In fact, that is what the behavioral treatment of all anxiety disorders is like. Clients must do things that are counterintuitive. They must head in what feels like the wrong direction, flying into the darkness.

When we are exposed to anything that makes us psychologically or physiologically uncomfortable, our natural reaction is to withdraw and escape or altogether avoid it. This is a natural tendency and has evolved to help us avoid danger. We are hard-wired to react this way—it is a survival mechanism, and it works.

Behavioral therapy (BT) involves going against the grain of that hard-wired, automatic, life-preserving reaction. At the core of behavior therapy for anxiety disorders is the idea that one needs to approach the very thing that makes one fearful—one has to "fly into the darkness" as long as it is not really dangerous. Although it seems counterintuitive and is extremely difficult, going against our natural instincts is exactly what we must do in order to overcome our fears. This is the battle with which all anxiety-disordered persons struggle, and this is their challenge.

At the core of behavior therapy for anxiety disorders is the idea that one needs to approach the very thing that makes one fearful—one has to "fly into the darkness."

The specific BT treatment for OCD is exposure therapy. This treatment requires the person with OCD to expose herself to the very thing or things that she most wants to run away from. It is like flying toward the dark part of the bee trap. The bee feels as if it's going in the wrong direction, but the truth is, it's the only way out. Likewise with OCD, exposure is the only way that clients can begin to feel some freedom from the fears and obsessions and the consequent compulsions associated with this disorder. It is the only way out of the trap of living the OCD life.

The challenge of utilizing exposure correctly in the treatment of OCD is a daunting one for clients. It is essentially about approaching or creating the very obsessive fear that they have always worked so hard to avoid. Once clients have confronted their fears, the next step is for them to refrain from engaging in compulsive rituals. Hence, the full name for this treatment, as noted in the Introduction, is exposure with response prevention, or ERP.

For some incarnations of this disorder, ERP appears straightforward. For example, for those individuals with contamination obsessions, it is about having them touch those things that they fear are contaminated and then refrain from washing their hands. For those individuals with "hit-and-run" checking compulsions (an obsession that one has unknowingly hit someone while driving a car, also referred to as motor vehicle accident OCD, or "MVA" OCD), ERP involves driving where there are people on the streets and then not driving back to check for bodies. Other manifestations of OCD, however, require more inventive applications of exposure treatment.

Although the bee trap presents a review of the basic concept behind exposure and response prevention, that is, approaching what was previously avoided, there are several important corollaries to this concept. It is not merely a matter of "flying into the darkness" that is required for one to escape from the OCD trap, it is also about knowing how to do it.

The common thread, the bedrock of the treatment, is the idea of approaching some aspect of the very thing clients want to avoid. It is going against one's own instincts, in a courageous and faithful attempt to gain freedom and control, and being the master of one's own body and mind as well as one's own destiny. However, there are some rules to the application of ERP for the treatment of OCD. A few of them are reviewed in the following stories.

Horror Movie

Micki and Arne are friends. Micki phones Arne and says, "Hey, Arne, let's go to the movies!" Arne agrees and is so excited that Micki invited him to go the movies that he forgets to ask what film they are going to see. They go to the movies and enter the theater, and Arne is so engrossed in his conversation with Micki that he is really not paying attention to anything else. And so even at this point he is unaware of what movie they're going to see.

They sit down and the movie starts. As it begins, Arne realizes that the film is one of the *Friday the 13th* franchise, and the first scene is intensely gory and gross, intended to shock the audience right away. Arne freaks.

He lets out a scream, stands and runs, and in a flash he is out of the theater and into the lobby. The moment Arne runs out of the theater, his emotional discomfort and physiological arousal decrease. He feels more comfortable and less afraid. This reinforces the escape response, making it more likely that he will use it again in the future.

At this point, if he does not reenter the theater, he would most likely not attempt to go see that movie again. He will have learned to expect that he would experience a bad reaction to that particular movie and would now avoid it, and very likely many things associated with it. This response is aptly termed the "avoidance response." Because of his fear and its consequent avoidance response, Arne is likely to avoid renting or purchasing the DVD of this movie when it comes out. If he was traumatized sufficiently by the experience, he may not feel comfortable entering that particular movie theater even to go see another movie, at least not for a while. He might even feel uncomfortable riding down the street that runs in front of the movie theater and end up avoiding that as well. Behavioral psychologists will easily identify this process as "generalization."

The escape response, because of the process of generalization, can result in extreme future avoidance patterns, which may interfere significantly with functioning. Running away from something feared usually results in a *short-term reduction* in the experience of that fear. However, it also results in a *long-term maintenance* of that fear and very often in an avoidance of many things associated with the original feared thing or experience.

Running away from something feared usually results in a short-term reduction *in the experience of that fear. However, it also results in a* long-term maintenance *of that fear.*

So Arne runs out of the theater, and Micki runs after him. Micki tells him, "Look it's really a great movie, I really want you to be there to share it with me." Arne says "No way!" And Micki responds, "I see that they sell those really big buckets of popcorn here in the lobby." And then adds, with a devilish grin and a sing-songy voice; "I'll buy you one of them if you come watch the movie with me …"

Well, Arne is a big snack food fan, and he agrees. They return to the theater and watch the movie together. Arne doesn't cover his eyes or ears: he really *watches* the movie with Micki. In moments, Arne is a mess. He screams and yells, gets really nauseous, sweats, and practically wets his pants. His heart is racing, his breathing is fast and shallow, and his muscles are trembling. He has an overall horrible time of it. Finally, the move is over, and Micki turns to him and asks, "Did you like it?" Arne responds, "No! That was awful! I was a mess!"

Micki smiles and says, "Oh, come on! It was great! Look, I really, really liked this movie. So much so that I'd really like to sit through it again right now! Whad'ya say?" The answer comes back, "No way am I doing that!" to which Micki responds, "They're selling those big chocolate malt balls in the lobby, …" and so off the two of them go to buy the malt balls and view the film a second time. At the end of the movie, Micki turns to Arne yet again to ask him to watch it a third time with her. Somehow she gets him to sit and watch through the entire film yet another time.

The day immediately after this marathon experience, Micki phones Arne and asks, "Hey what'cha doin'?" to which Arne replies, "Nothing much." Micki, in a challenging voice exclaims, "Come on, let's go to the movies again!" And so they go to the same movie again, and they watch it three more times. On the third day she calls him up yet again, and Arne, who has never been much of a socialite, once again has nothing else planned for the day. Off they go together and watch that same film again, and again, and again. Nine times now.

It's a four-day holiday weekend, and they do the same thing on that last day. So they have now seen the movie a total of twelve times.

Consider this question: Is Arne's reaction to the twelfth viewing of this film going to be the same as his reaction the very first time he viewed it? No, of course not; it is now completely different. He doesn't have the negative physical reactions that he did the first time he saw it. Why? *Because he has gotten used to it.* He has become *desensitized* and *habituated*, meaning he has now become less sensitive to the movie. An originally novel experience has become more habit-like after repeated exposures.

As a result of habituation and desensitization, Arne no longer reacts to the movie in the same way. He may never get to the point where he *likes* the movie the way that Micki does, but he most probably will ultimately find himself bored by it. It's a safe bet that he won't freak out over it the way he did during his first viewing.

It is also noteworthy that Arne didn't need to *do anything* to become desensitized to the horror movie, except to watch it repeatedly within a relatively short period of time. He didn't practice relaxation exercises, he didn't examine his thought processes and create alternative internal self-talk that would help reduce his fear and anxiety. He just watched the movie over and over and over again. Exposure, in and of itself, has the power to move one from a place of fear to a place of no fear, or at least a place of significantly less fear.

The OCD Connection

Exposure, in and of itself, has the power to move one from a place of fear to a place of no fear, or at least a place of significantly less fear.

Earlier the bee trap story illustrated how approaching the things that we fear is essential to overcoming that fear and that the only way to escape from the "trap" is to face fears head on and to "fly toward the darkness." The horror movie story illustrates the notion that we must do this repeatedly, exposing ourselves a multitude of times to that which we fear, in order to create the reduction in fear via the processes of habituation and desensitization.

The good news is that this process gets easier with repetition. The bad news is that it is just so damn awful that very first time! Clients may listen to the horror movie story and become terrified. They may claim that what Arne had to go through the first time he was exposed to the movie sounded terrible and that they can't envision themselves ever being able to endure such torture. Even if they accept the idea that flying into the darkness repeatedly will ultimately free them of the fears that imprison them, they may be unwilling to subject themselves to the physiological and psychological discomfort that Arne experienced in the initial stages of exposure when he watched the movie for the very first time. They just don't want to accept that level of distress. The good news is, they do not have to in order to successfully challenge the OCD, because there is an alternative to throwing oneself headlong into an intense exposure experience as Arne did at the horror movie.

Swimming Pool

It's a very hot summer day. Before you is a freezing-cold, unheated in-ground swimming pool. There are two strategies for entering this pool. The first is the running "cannon ball dive," where you run toward the pool and, as you reach its edge, fling your body over the water, tuck your knees tightly toward your chest, and plunge yourself deep into the frigid waters. You scream for about thirty seconds, and before you know it, you have become acclimated to the pool temperature and enjoy the refreshing coolness of the water.

Alternatively, you can go in very gently. You can enter at the shallow end to where the stairs are, and tiptoe in. This way, your feet get cold, the water feels like it is freezing, but in a few moments you get used to it, and it doesn't feel quite so bad. You then slowly walk a little further in and your lower legs get cold, so you stop there for a minute or so and wait for yourself to again get used to the temperature. You proceed slowly and cautiously in this manner, and ultimately, you're completely submerged in the water, where you eventually end up getting used to it. Compared to jumping or diving in all at once, the shock to your system is not nearly as great when you go in gradually in this manner, but it's spread out over a longer period of time. The process is called gradual or graduated exposure.

In the horror movie story, graduated exposure might have involved Arne first looking at and studying small black-and-white still photos from the movie. He would do this until his anxiety dropped significantly from its initial high point, and then he would graduate to looking at larger color photographs of the film. Once he was able to view these photos without severe anxiety, he would move on to watching small clips of the film over and over again until he could watch each clip without undue anxiety. Other steps might then include watching the film at home with friends, with the lights on, then watching it alone, then alone with the lights off, and so on.

The OCD Connection

In treatment for OCD, the client chooses his own pace in the application of exposure. Persons struggling with OCD, or any anxiety disorder for that matter, often have a sense of not being "in control" of their own physiological, cognitive, and behavioral experience. Explaining to OCD clients very early in treatment that the pace and intensity of exposure therapy will be determined largely by them helps them to feel less apprehensive about moving forward and reassures them that they will have control over the therapeutic process.

Explaining to OCD clients very early in treatment that the pace and intensity of exposure therapy will be determined largely by them helps them to feel less apprehensive about moving forward.

How quickly one wants to go through the process is measured against how much discomfort one is willing to tolerate. Choose a slower, graduated exposure, and the discomfort levels will be more moderate, but the entire process will take longer. Choose a more intense exposure, and the anxiety is likewise more intense, but the process toward desensitization is shorter in duration—clients will get where they want to go more quickly.

So, although ERP requires repeated attempts at flying into the darkness, clients can actually fly at a controlled, slowed rate, so that they may better manage anxiety levels every step of the way.

Toronto, at the CN Tower

My son plays ice hockey. He lives and breathes the game. He is a fan in the full sense of the word, in that I believe he qualifies as a true fanatic.

So when he was 11 years old, we made sure that part of our summer vacation travels included some time in Toronto, where my son could visit the Hockey Hall of Fame.

While in Toronto, we also visited one of the other big tourist attractions, the CN tower. At over 1800 feet tall, 181 stories in all, the CN tower is the tallest man made structure in all the Americas (as of this writing). The tower looks like a very tall cylinder that pierces a large circular structure about four-fifths of the way to the top. Visitors enter the tower at the bottom of the cylinder, which consists of nothing more than six elevators that take you up to the main structure.

When you exit the elevator, you can walk around the main structure and look out the windows, which serve essentially as an observation tower, or you can eat in the restaurant located up there. There is a section of the floor in the observation deck at the top of the tower, shaped in a square and covering an area of approximately 16 feet by 16 feet, that is entirely replaced by glass. Although you can walk around it, the challenge to visitors is clear: "Dare you walk across this glass, where you can clearly see 113 stories below you?"

I was intrigued by this challenge and so walked up to the edge of where the glass began. The glass floor section itself was made up of several glass panels, each about 4 feet wide and 4 feet long, separated by steel beams a couple of inches in width. I looked down and could see the cars hundreds of feet below, looking smaller than toys, and I found myself experiencing a curious reaction. My heart was pounding wildly, and I could clearly hear the sound of blood rushing in my ears. My muscles were extremely tight, I felt just a touch light-headed, and my stomach felt as if it was turning on itself ever so slightly. It was a little hard to breathe. Essentially I was experiencing a very mild panic attack.

Now, I spend most of my work days urging people to fly into the darkness and face their own fears, so it seemed unfair that I should ignore this challenge and walk around the section of floor made of glass. I decided I was going to go for it, despite my feelings of fear and panic. I began slowly, by placing one foot on one of the steel beams that separated two glass panels. I slowly shifted my weight onto that foot, and stood there for a few seconds, feeling my anxiety climb, even as I thought to myself, "I don't really believe there is much of a chance at all that the glass would fail and I will fall through!" This contradiction—that I could be relatively sure in my mind that I was really OK, yet experience an incredibly intense physiological reaction as if my body were not so convinced of its safety—is often echoed by people who have OCD when they discuss facing their fears in exposure therapy.

I continued by lifting my foot slowly off the solid floor outside of the glassed section and placing it next to my other foot on the beam. My eyes were closed, and I waited for my heart to calm down a bit before I opened them. First, I glanced forward, looking at the other visitors who were challenging themselves in a like manner. Most of the younger kids, mind you, were running across the glass section screaming with delight, or jumping up and down on the glass! The adults all seemed to be struggling in one way or another. After I got used to standing on the beam, I looked down, seeing the view directly beneath the beam. Again, my panic reaction started, and I needed some time before I could move to the next step.

My children, who had themselves already mastered this challenge and crossed the glass floor, started to complain that they wanted to move on, but I was bent on completing this "exposure" before I could leave. I slowly lifted my foot again, placed it in the middle of a glass panel, and closed my eyes as I ever so slowly shifted my weight to it. I lifted my second foot off the beam and again, very slowly, placed it next to the first one on the glass panel. The level of anxiety was intense. However, just as occurs during an exposure exercise in therapy, my increase in anxiety was followed by a marked decrease as a result of habituation.

Eventually I was able to cross the glass floor without undue anxiety, at which time my kids were physically pulling at me so we could move on and leave the Tower. The process took 22 minutes for me from beginning to end (I glanced at my watch as soon as I made the decision to take on the challenge). I wanted to have a very specific experience of facing fears that I would be able to share with my clients—to be more sensitive to what it was that I was encouraging my clients to experience every day in therapy. I also took on this challenge because I expected to be successful and just wanted to feel good about conquering a fear.

The OCD Connection

As difficult as it was, my exposure experience at the CN Tower was different from that of most of those clients with OCD who engage in

ERP, especially when they do so for the first time. The difference was that I had complete trust in the process. Before I even started, I was certain that I would be able to walk across that glass floor if I gave it enough time and if I challenged myself in small steps. I knew exactly what to expect: heightened anxiety each time I increased the level of the challenge, followed by a relatively quick drop once I got acclimated. I was certain of this because I had seen it happen literally hundreds of times with clients over the almost twenty years that I had been doing ERP work in therapy. This state of certainty, I believe, allowed the process of acclimation, or what is sometimes called desensitization or habituation, to occur so rapidly for me. I "threw myself" with abandon into the process, confident that despite what my anxiety and my body's reactions were telling me, I was indeed safe, and these feelings of danger were transient.

In therapy, as clients successfully navigate through the exposure process for certain OCD symptoms, they will often move through the process more quickly when they later challenge *other* OCD symptoms. This is true especially if the initial level of anxiety triggered by these other symptoms is of the same level as that for the symptoms already subjected to ERP. Simply put, clients become more confident that they will be successful, with the result that the process of habituation/desensitization is accelerated.

As clients successfully navigate through the exposure process for certain OCD symptoms, they will often move through the process more quickly when they later challenge other *OCD symptoms.*

Once an individual becomes more confident that the process of ERP really works, and that he can be successful whenever trying to conquer fear, then something changes. Situations that trigger OCD anxiety, rather than also triggering the thought, "How do I avoid this?" (consequently leading to avoidant behavior), instead elicit a knee-jerk reaction of something like, "Ah! Another opportunity to show OCD who is the boss!" resulting in taking up the challenge of facing the fear and flying into the darkness.

This is exactly what happened with me at the CN Tower. Because I was determined and, more importantly, *confident* that I would be successful, a situation that triggered in me even very high anxiety led me naturally to *want* to challenge myself and fly into the darkness and face my fears. This *confidence* and trust in the ERP process is key to success in therapy.

Monsters under the Bed

Imagine that you are eight years old. You're lying on your bed in your room waiting to fall asleep. The lights are out, but even with your nightlight on, you are terrified. Maybe it was that science fiction TV show your parents told you that you probably shouldn't be watching. Maybe it was that third helping of chocolate cake with the pink icing that you had during snack time. Whatever it was, there you are, lying in your bed, terrified. Terrified that there are monsters under your bed! Purple ones, green ones, ooey-gooey ones—all kinds of nasty monsters! You try to listen closely, and you are sure that you can hear them breathing.

Now, the truth is, you are pretty sure that there really aren't monsters under your bed. But it really *feels* like there could be. The only way to know for sure is to bend over the edge of the bed and look underneath. But dare you do such a thing? What if—there it is, the famous question of "what if?" familiar to all persons with OCD—what if they really *are* there?! Maybe that's what they're waiting for: for you to bend over the side of the bed so that they can bite your head off! You are not really sure you want to find that out. So there you lie, waiting. As long as you don't look and check it out, they could be down there, you can never tell. But it is so *scary* to think of leaning over and looking that you feel like you are paralyzed. So you hardly move a muscle, trying not to breathe too loudly.

A few minutes pass, and you think you're just going to have to look. You begin to think of what the other kids will be saying in school when they hear you were eaten by monsters in your bedroom. You think about how your younger brother will commandeer all your favorite computer games and electronic toys. You think about being tired and just wanting to go to sleep already!

You decide to go for it. One … Two …Three … GO!

Nothing but dust bunnies and an empty bag of pretzels.

Whew! You're safe! You relax now, thinking how silly you were. You feel confident that no monster will get you from under that bed of yours. Now … what about that slightly open closet?

The OCD Connection

At the core of exposure and response prevention in the treatment of OCD is the idea that one needs to approach the very thing that one fears in an attempt to prove to oneself that there is, in all probability, nothing to fear.

For those with checking compulsions, for instance, the fear is usually "what if I *don't* check?" Therefore, the exposure is to not check. In this story, however, since the fear is "what if I *do* check?" *that* becomes the thing we *must* do. Telling this to a person with OCD, however, is sometimes like trying to tell an eight-year-old that he should "just look under the bed!"

As always, whether we are talking about monsters or OCD (as if there were a difference between the two!), clients overcome their fears by challenging them directly and moving toward the very thing that they find most frightening. Look under the bed!

I have from time to time treated young heterosexual men who have OC obsessions that make them wonder whether they might be gay. This is actually a relatively common OC obsession. I can be pretty sure that these young men are in fact heterosexual for several reasons, not the least of which is that they usually report having only heterosexual fantasies that lead to sexual arousal, and they deny having had any sexual arousal in response to intrusive homosexual fantasies, which elicit only anxiety.

Clients overcome their fears by challenging them directly and moving toward the very thing that they find most frightening.

Exposure involves, of course, the weird intervention of asking these clients to tell themselves that they *are* gay, often by having them write down that they are gay on a piece of paper and carrying it around with them in their pockets. More intense exposure exercises may include looking at pictures of men in magazines and trying to imagine them within a sexual context or, with persons of legal age, going to a gay bar or looking at gay pornography.

The exposure does prove to these individuals with OCD that they really are not gay. But it is important to note that as long as they avoid exposure and instead try to reason with themselves that they are not gay, the doubt of what's "under that bed" will haunt them, and they will continue to fear that maybe they really are. In fact the avoidance itself functions as a sort of "proof" that they are gay. Otherwise why would they be working so hard to avoid thinking about it?

Teaching the Radio

One of the benefits of living in between two major cities, as I do, is that you can access the radio stations of both. With the advent of computer access to radio stations from all over the country, this is no longer of particular consequence, but just a short time ago, it presented a distinct advantage. Sometimes, however, this presented certain frustrations as well.

For example, there was one particular radio station, a public station out of one of the universities in Philadelphia, that produced a signal that was strong enough to reach my area, but only barely. Depending on exactly where you lived, you might find yourself just on the outskirts of the station's transmission range, and the signal would tend to go in and out depending on where you happened to drive your car, the weather conditions, or the time of the day.

This radio station constantly battled with a smaller, more local radio station, which had nearly the same bandwidth. Both stations would sometimes come through at the same time, and at other times neither would come through, and you would get only static. To add to the frustration, sometimes the most obscure variables seemed to affect the strength of the signal. You might find that if you stood in a certain part of the room where the radio was located, the signal would come in more clearly, or that if you held your hand on the radio you could serve as a human antenna, and the station would play louder and clearer as a result. What could really be infuriating, however, was if someone moved the radio dial to listen to another station. Then you would need to fiddle with the dial for a long time to find just the right frequency again.

However, if you were a true fan of this particular station, and you had a little patience, you would be unexpectedly rewarded. It seemed that if you kept the radio tuned long enough to the frequency most suited to picking up the Philadelphia station, something remarkable would occur. Your radio would eventually tune in more easily to this station, and it would seem to require less effort and acrobatics to regain the signal if it got lost or interrupted. The competing local radio signal would no longer interrupt the transmission of the desired station.

Persons versed in electronics are sometimes familiar with this phenomenon, and they will casually tell you that your radio had actually "gotten better" at locking onto the signal because you had tuned into it so frequently. They will explain that your radio had actually "learned" to better pick up this hard-to-reach station because the repeated movement of the electrons through its hardware had essentially made an easy path of less resistance, allowing for the radio signal to come through more strongly. You may find this explanation to be completely implausible, but it was reminiscent of a similar theory about brain functioning, memory, and skills building.

The OCD Connection

According to the theory, every time we learn something completely new, say, playing an instrument like the piano for the first time, we create an actual, physical pathway between certain neurons in our brains. As we practice our new skill, the neural signals begin to travel more freely and with less resistance along this pathway, allowing for greater strength of signal with less effort on the part of the learner.

Think of trying to make your way through an area of overgrown, virgin jungle. The first time through, you would need to machete your way, slowly and with great effort, to get from one side of the jungle to the other. However, as you traverse this path back and forth, over and over again, the path becomes easier to negotiate. The more it is used, the more welcoming it is to the traveler. Take a vacation from using the path, and it starts to overgrow again, making it less hospitable and more difficult to walk through.

You may question if either of these metaphors, the electronic circuits of your radio or the neural pathways in the brain, is an accurate representation for the processes they supposedly explain. Nevertheless, they represent an interesting dynamic that can be used in OCD work.

When clients first start to do exposure work in combating an OCD obsession, the anxiety can be extremely high. With repeated exposures, it becomes easier. This we know from our discussions of desensitization and habituation. But in addition to the anxiety reaction becoming less pronounced with repeated trials of exposure, something else changes. The effort required to even *think* along the lines of exposure, of "flying into the darkness," diminishes. It becomes more automatic for clients to respond to an obsession with thoughts of "How do I challenge this?" as opposed to "How do I escape from this experience of anxiety?"

According to this idea, exposure trials become less uncomfortable with repetition, not only because clients "get used" to the situation, resulting in desensitization and a resulting drop in anxiety, but also because they more naturally think along the lines of engaging in

Exposure trials become less uncomfortable with repetition.

exposure-type behavior to begin with. It becomes less effortful to focus one's energies on engaging in battle via the paradox of approach rather than avoidance. In this way we can imagine that the repeated employment of exposure therapy to different situations will result in the enhancement of neural pathways in the brain, in the same way that learning the piano, painstakingly slow and requiring so much effort in the beginning, ultimately flows smoothly, quickly, and effortlessly with practice.

This creates a wonderful cycle that can catapult the OC sufferer into relative wellness; she more spontaneously chooses an exposure response to challenge an obsessive thought, which itself serves to initiate a process that lowers the anxiety that she experiences. The practice her brain gets in thinking this way, as well as the reinforcement she experiences via the reduction in anxiety through ERP, both serve to make it easier and more likely for her to spontaneously choose an exposure response to the next obsessive thought that the OCD throws at her. Like the seasoned pianist who sits down on the bench and, without any music sheets to guide her, effortlessly plays a classical piece, the seasoned OCD challenger chooses a proactive, aggressive exposure response at the first sign of an obsession and barely considers how to neutralize the anxiety via escape, avoidance, or ritual.

You now have a set of stories that will help you to introduce exposure work to your clients and their significant others. By defining the mechanics of this treatment protocol and addressing the essentials of how it works, you set the stage for the explanation of the more subtle aspects of this treatment.

3

The Nuts and Bolts of Exposure Therapy

The stories in this chapter go beyond the definition of what exposure therapy is and address some of the finer details of this intervention, including looking at how exposure therapy is organized, setting up a hierarchy, and reviewing the behavioral concepts of generalization, conditioning behaviors, and associations. In addition, a good number of these stories address concerns that clients often voice as they learn what will be required of them for successful exposure treatment, such as whether they are capable of facing their fears, following through with homework, or overcoming plateaus in their progress. Other stories in this chapter address engaging in exposure therapy with the application of humor or adopting a passive-aggressive attitude.

Flossing

As a youngster, I went regularly to my family dentist. At every six-month checkup he would say to me, "Allen, you really need to be flossing more often." He would give me a little scare talk about gum disease and send me out of the office with one of those little round tins with some sample floss in it. I'd get really motivated, make a commitment to myself that I was going to get serious about flossing, and off I'd go, home to floss.

I would start flossing diligently that first night, but the technique is difficult if you haven't been doing it much. It involves a lot of hand-eye coordination. You need to really know your proper angles to get that floss where you want it, and some of the spaces between your teeth can be really tight. And I found that somehow my elbows would get in the way.

I would struggle considerably with this first flossing attempt and found that it would take me something like five full minutes just to do one quadrant of my mouth. I'd feel spastic and clumsy, stupid and frustrated, and I'd inevitably end up saying to myself, "Forget it! I don't have time for this!" and I wouldn't floss again until the next time I saw my dentist, six months later, at which time the story would repeat itself. This circular process went on for years.

Eventually, I went away to college and found a new dentist. On my first visit with him, he gave me the same "You need to be flossing more" speech. I told him the same story that I just shared with you, admitting that in all likelihood, I would likely fail in completing a flossing regimen.

His response was a little bit surprising. He told me, "Allen, this is what I want you to do. Here's the floss. I want you to go home. Floss for sixty seconds, then stop. Even if you only do one tooth, stop after sixty seconds. The next day, start with the same tooth, and do sixty seconds again. That's all."

I decided, "Well, I could do *that*!" No big deal, a piece of cake really. And so, that night, I flossed for sixty seconds. The next day I flossed for sixty seconds again, and what ended up happening was that I got a little better at it. Within a couple of days, I could do several teeth in sixty seconds. In just a few more days, sixty seconds allowed me to do about a quarter of my mouth.

Around that time it dawned on me that I had probably developed enough skill to be able to floss my whole mouth in under four minutes. "Well, I can do *four minutes!*" I said to myself. And so I did four minutes. Soon I was able to floss my entire mouth in under two minutes. That was twenty-five years ago, I haven't stopped flossing yet, and I have great teeth, thank you very much.

This new approach allowed me to interrupt my previous pattern of behavior and jump over that wall of resistance and avoidance by realizing that I didn't have to do "the whole thing," at least not at first. I just had to do this little tiny part. Sixty seconds. That's where I needed to start. As the the ancient Chinese proverb teaches, the journey of a thousand miles begins with a single step.

The OCD Connection

In the treatment of OCD, the art of the therapy is being able to figure out how intense the first exposure experiences should be. The goal is to trigger a sense significant anxiety, because if you start too slowly, the client doesn't have the experience of increased anxiety followed by a decrease via habituation. On the other hand, if the client "bites off more than he can chew," and the initial exposure experience that you are prescribing is too intense, you risk the possibility that the client will become overwhelmed and terminate treatment.

Ultimately, the decision is in the hands of the client. Typically, there is initial apprehension, and the idea of challenging the OCD by touching something, or not washing, or somehow resisting a compulsion is experienced as an impossible task. In such cases, you may invoke the dentist story. You can essentially say to the client, "OK, if you can't do *that*, what *can* you do?" In this way, the client doesn't feel coerced or forced to engage in a specific exposure experience that might undermine his sense of power and control in the treatment process, but at the same time, he is still held accountable to *do something* specific to challenge his OCD.

You can essentially say to the client, "OK, if you can't do that, *what* can *you do?"*

Principles of Weight Lifting

Steve lifts weights. He likes to bench press, an exercise that has a person lying on his back on a workout bench and lifting up a set of barbells directly overhead. "One of the things I've noticed," reports Steve, "is that no matter how many weeks I bench press 150 pounds, it still requires what feels like the same amount of effort. I struggle just as much each time I exercise, and it doesn't seem to be getting easier. I seem only to be maintaining my strength, not increasing it."

Steve goes to the gym and discusses his frustration with the coaches there. Later, Steve reports, "I found out something very interesting. Even though I was still struggling while bench pressing 150 pounds, I moved up to 160 pounds, as the coaches suggested. It was much harder, but I was able to do it. I did find, however, that after increasing the weight for about a week, when I went back and tried 150 pounds again, it was a breeze! It felt as if it took relatively no effort at all!"

The OCD Connection

This conclusion of Steve's brings to mind an OCD issue. When doing exposure work, it seems as if clients never truly get beyond their anxiety about something until they go to the next step in their exposure hierarchy.

For example, assume you are treating a client with the OCD fear of accidentally hitting someone with her car without realizing it, a common obsession called, "hit and run OCD," or "motor vehicle accident" ("MVA OCD"). You assist your client in constructing an exposure hierarchy and begin a series of exercises going up the hierarchy. She gets to the point where she can drive alone on a fairly quiet road during the day; however, she finds that, in spite of engaging in this behavior repeatedly, she continues to experience significant anxiety. Why isn't her anxiety lessening?

The answer lies with our weight-lifting friend. When your client first attempted this level of exposure, chances are the anxiety level was extremely high. After a few trials, however, her anxiety leveled off. Still, it remained, and she hasn't been able to lower it further. The intervention of choice is to go to the *next* step on the hierarchy, say, driving alone at *night* on a quiet road. Initially here, too, the anxiety will be extreme, but it will soon level off. Once she has reached this point, if she now goes *back* to driving alone on a quiet road during the day, it will seem relatively easy.

The intervention of choice is to go to the next step on the hierarchy.

You may employ this weight-lifting story to assist your client in taking that next step, even while she continues to struggle in her present level of hierarchal exposure. In so doing you assist her in breaking free of a hierarchal plateau, which may generate a lack of faith on her part, and consequently a loss of motivation and momentum.

Flying Pebbles on the Highway

At around the time I was in graduate school, I was driving along the highway and came up behind a large dump truck traveling in the middle lane. It was full to capacity with small stones, pebbles really, and appeared to have come from a quarry. The top of the truck was open, but it had a material cover which was tied down at its four corners and ran across the top of the vehicle so as to prevent the stones from falling out as the truck traveled. One corner of the cover had come undone, and was flapping in the wind as the truck raced on at highway speed.

As a result, pebbles were jarred loose from the top of the truck, and a steady stream of them was left in the wake of the dump truck as it sped on.

Unaware of this situation, I approached the rear of the truck, and my windshield was struck by one of these pebbles, cracking the glass slightly. My body reacted with a jolt, and I found that my eyes shut tightly, completely out of my control, though only for what was probably a fraction of a second. This response occurred automatically, and without any thought. It felt as if I had absolutely no control over it.

I shared this experience with my roommate at the time, and we decided to try an experiment. We filled some balloons with water and decided to see if we could train ourselves to remain unresponsive to an oncoming projectile. I sat in the driver's seat of my car, and he threw the balloons at regular intervals at the front windshield, directly at my face behind the glass. I found that, surprisingly, within as little as three balloon throws, I was able to remain motionless, without even closing my eyes, in response to the oncoming water balloon.

With just a few throws I essentially unlearned an automatic response that I had believed was hard-wired into my brain as a self-protective mechanism. After all, this was an animal-level, instinctual phenomenon, a result of many millennia of evolutionary development. That I could turn off such a seemingly involuntary response seemed quite surprising.

The OCD Connection

The experiment, of course, was a demonstration of habituation in action. While three balloon throws with one person obviously falls short of a true scientific experiment which could serve to validate any theory, still, the results seemed to suggest that with repeated exposure experiences, even the most primal of our instinctual responses can be altered. And so it may be with fear: another primal, instinctual response.

With repeated exposure experiences, even the most primal of our instinctual responses can be altered.

Repeated exposure to a stimulus that normally elicits a fear reaction in a person (whether an automatic eye blink in response to an apparently oncoming projectile or an increase in respiration or heart rate in response to exposure to perceived contamination) will result in the reduction or even the elimination of that response if the initial stimulus is ultimately determined to be benign. If I learn through repeated exposure, not only intellectually, but again, *experientially*, that the thing I am afraid of is not really dangerous, then I can learn not to be afraid of it, and my body can learn not to automatically respond with physiological reactions in an attempt to protect me. And so exposure work gets easier with repetition.

When clients report a lack of faith that their intense fear reactions will subside even with repeated exposure, when they share that they cannot comprehend better controlling their compulsive rituals no matter how many exposure trials they attempt, you may invoke this story as a way of demonstrating that even the most basic of human reactions, automatic behaviors designed to self-protect, can often come under our conscious control with repeated practice.

Under the Couch

I moved into an off-campus house when attending graduate school. This house, rented to successive groups of students, had obviously seen many years of neglect and abuse. The walls were pretty badly marked up, the kitchen floor was dingy and badly scratched, and the carpets throughout were soiled and stained.

Students ourselves, my roommate and I were not interested in spending a great deal of time and effort to rehabilitate the house, especially because we knew we would not be living there more than a few semesters ourselves. However, our threshold for tolerating high levels of dirt and grime was much less than that of the previous renters, and so we proceeded to spend our initial days cleaning up the place as best we could.

We gave the rooms a fresh coat of paint and scrubbed the kitchen floors, and cleaned the place thoroughly. Our biggest challenge, however, was to clean the carpet. It was there, on that carpet, where we would entertain our guests, or sit and watch TV in the living room, so it was essential that it be comfortably clean. We rented a carpet-cleaning machine from the local supermarket and set about bringing new life to the colors and fibers under our feet.

Once this had been done, the carpet looked great. Nearly all the stains were gone, and most of the gray had been taken out, leaving a bright, blue/green color on our floor. For the next few weeks, we sprawled comfortably on the carpet each day, feeling secure in the fact that we had cleaned it thoroughly and that our bodies were against a pristine surface that had been rid of all debris left by previous tenants of the house.

Now it so happened that there was a rather large couch on one side of the TV room, and we had decided not to bother to move it when we cleaned the carpet, in part because our several attempts to do so nearly resulted in us both developing hernias, since the thing weighed more than any couch had a right to. We decided it must have been made of lead because it was completely immovable; but in any event, we also assumed that nobody would see under the couch anyway, and so, the carpet remained uncleaned beneath the huge couch except for what we could reach with a special vacuum attachment.

Things were fine until, about two months later, when my roommate inherited a sound system from an older sibling that could be hooked up to the TV, creating a "surround-sound" effect. We then needed to reconfigure the furniture in the room to accommodate the new audio equipment. This meant moving the couch from one side of the room to the other, which we did with a help of a few friends. Although this allowed for better viewing and listening to music and TV, it created a completely unanticipated problem.

We had expected that the carpeting under the couch would be dirty, but were shocked, to find that it was in fact, *clean*! And not just clean, but pristine, as if it were just laid down, having been protected for years by the couch. This now created a new problem: the rest of the carpeting, which we had deluded ourselves into thinking was pretty clean, now looked worn and filthy by comparison!

What is interesting about this story (and the point of telling it) is that it demonstrates the concept that what once appeared perfectly clean can suddenly appear as rather dirty when compared to something even cleaner. Perhaps you yourself have changed residences, and noticed that the wall you thought had a perfectly acceptable level of cleanliness looked suddenly dark and dirty once you moved the pictures hanging on it, and you could then compare the wall that you had always seen to the "pristine" squares that had been protected by the pictures and their frames. It is this concept that plays a crucial role in the development of proper behavioral interventions for the treatment of OCD.

The OCD Connection

In exposure and response prevention (ERP), the client is exposed to certain stimuli that provoke obsessional thinking, while he works on preventing (or interrupting, changing, or delaying) his response (the ritual or compulsion) to the obsession. The nature of the ERP intervention varies widely with the specific OCD problem and the particular individual who has the OCD. The challenge for the therapist is to help create the ERP intervention that will be the most effective for that person and for that particular form of OCD.

The challenge for the therapist is to help create the ERP intervention that will be the most effective for that person and for that particular form of OCD.

Let's look at the OCD problem of contamination and a compulsive need to wash and clean. This is probably the best well known of all the OCD obsessive-compulsive cycles, and so it seems like a good OCD presentation to explore. For most "washers," as they are sometimes called, it is not so much touching a thing that feels "dirty" or, as is the preferred adjective, "contaminated," that is the main challenge. For many of these people, it is the idea that they need to wash (usually with some kind of specific behavioral ritual) in order to "cleanse" themselves before they can touch anything else, lest they "spread" the contamination to other things. Their fear is that if they spread the contamination to these other things, they will then need to either go through some kind of rigorous ritual to properly clean those things, avoid them totally, or wash immediately each time after coming into contact with them.

But just touching something that is contaminated and not washing afterward, although a good start in the exposure hierarchy, is not the ultimate goal. The goal is to get contaminated, not wash, and, in the state of contamination, *spread that contamination* by going around touching all kinds of things that had not previously been contaminated. Literally, a client would contaminate himself by touching, even embracing, a contaminated item, say a book bag that had touched the floor of a public restroom, and then would go around touching the furniture, the kitchen table, the bedding, and so on. Although a person may need to do this slowly, adding only one or two things to be touched every time he has an ERP session, ultimately the goal is to be able to walk around in a contaminated state touching just about anything and everything that one would normally come in contact with in the home over the course of the day.

By not going back and cleaning these items, and allowing himself to touch these items as needed, the client will find that, after repeated exposures, the intensity of the experience of contamination fades. He himself, and the things he is touching, no longer feel particularly dirty. And so through the process of desensitization/habituation, he no longer has to avoid, no longer has to wash, indeed no longer even has to think about any of these things, as is the case with the rest of us who do not have OCD.

But there are often times that a particular complication arises. A good many people will often refuse to contaminate certain things in the home. This is true even if they have contaminated a good number of things already. Sometimes it is the pillow on the bed, or the cutlery in the kitchen, the bathroom towel, the toothbrush, or the clothes in the closet or in the chest of drawers.

"I have done so much already; can't I just leave those things alone? I like the sense that they have been 'untouched' by the contaminant," is the kind of thing you might hear them say.

Of course, they can *choose* to do that, but it would be a mistake. It would be a mistake for the same reason that the carpet looked clean only until we saw it next to the protected carpet underneath the couch. Things appear only as clean as in relationship to the things around them. As long as one set of clothes, one pillow, or just one item in the kitchen remains "pure" and uncontaminated, all the other things that the person has touched and exposed to the contaminant will still feel somewhat contaminated, even after long periods of time and repeated exposures. This is because there are still "pure" items in the home which contrast to the contaminated items.

Assume the items in a client's home are ranked on a scale of 0–10, where 0 is completely free of contamination and 10 is the most contaminated, and therefore the most difficult to touch. Once *everything* is contaminated, then everything essentially becomes a "0" in our 0–10 exposure hierarchy. This becomes our new baseline, our starting point for evaluating how dirty something feels. But as long as you have one item that is completely uncontaminated, that item becomes the baseline "0," and so everything else becomes a "1" or more.

As a therapist, when your OCD client struggles with executing the "touch and spread" form of ERP, and entertains the idea of leaving some parts of her or his life uncontaminated, invoking the story of "under the couch" can serve to help explain why it is preferable to touch *everything.*

Boot Camp

There are two basic approaches to applying exposure and response prevention when constructing a treatment protocol for OCD. Both start with the identification of something that triggers an OCD obsession, such as a doorknob triggering the obsession that maybe it is contaminated. This leads to anxiety, which in this case, results in an avoidant behavior—not touching the doorknob, waiting for someone else to open the door, or using a paper towel or shirt sleeve as an indirect way of not touching the doorknob. The ERP approach involves challenging the anxiety in some way and, through a step by step approach, altering one's behavior just a little bit each time so that one is more closely approximating nonavoidant behavior. Through repeated exposures, one should get to the point where the behavior feels essentially "normal," and in this case, the person can open the door by grasping the doorknob directly without any concurrent anxiety.

In all these ways ERP of any kind is essentially the same. But there are differences in the ways in which ERP, as a treatment intervention, can be *organized.* One way, which may be called *serendipitous exposure,* is essentially challenging oneself to take as many opportunities as possible over the course of one's day to engage in ERP. Essentially, it is saying to oneself, "Over the course of every day, every time I need to open a door, rather than engage in avoidant behavior, I will change my behavior in some way in order to challenge the OCD obsession." This might mean taking the first step in exposure by opening the door barehanded and then waiting a certain period of time before washing. Alternatively, it could mean first opening the door by grasping the back part of the doorknob or handle, which may be perceived as less contaminated because typically people are less likely to touch those parts when opening the door. Another way one could start would be to use only one part of one's hand (say, just the finger tips, or just the palm) when opening the door. Or it could mean choosing less challenging doors to start with, and working one's way up to the inside handle of a bathroom door. The contract, the commitment, is to try to be aware of every time one needs to open a door and use that opportunity to *not* engage in one's typical OCD ritual or avoidant behavior. Over time, as the new behavior becomes desensitized and less anxiety producing, the person would increase the challenge, until the door could be opened without any anxiety.

Serendipitous exposure does not need to be limited to a single situation as with the doorknob. The contract a person makes, either with him- or herself, a family member or friend, or with a therapist, could be more broad, such as stating, "Whenever, over the course of a day, I find myself needing to come in contact with *anything* that I perceive to be contaminated, I will change my behavior in some way to challenge my OCD." Serendipitous exposure is very effective because it is a "real life" exposure, that is, it is exposure in the real world. It is limited, however, by circumstance and opportunity. What if my home itself is not contaminated and I happen to have no need or desire to go out one day? No ERP takes place. What if I only really have to open a door when I enter my workplace and when I leave it? Then my ERP for the day is limited to two, or maybe four, exposures for the entire day.

The term *serendipitous* is defined as "the accidental discovery of something pleasant, valuable, or useful." Pleasantness aside, serendipitous exposure is dependent on stumbling across a useful and valuable exposure opportunity over the course of one's day. It is limited by how many things you do, how many places you go, and ultimately, how many OCD triggers you happen to come across. This is why, in working with OCD clients, CBT therapists will often contract to do "formalized" or "structured" ERP. The following metaphor may be shared with clients when introducing the concept of structured ERP.

Serendipitous exposure is dependent on stumbling across a useful and valuable exposure opportunity over the course of one's day.

Think of those professions that require a person to perform his or her job under extreme emotionally volatile conditions. These might include emergency medical technicians, police officers, firefighters, or soldiers. These people have to do their jobs while people may be dying around them, or while they themselves are in danger. Their own lives, or the lives of others, or both, may be at risk in the very moments that they have to execute the skills of their profession.

These professionals are all trained in similar ways. They learn a set of specific skills, and then, once these have been learned, and usually before they ever get a chance to actually apply any of these skills in real world situations, they drill, and drill, and drill. This is probably most self-evident when a soldier enters boot camp in the armed forces. This intense introductory period of several weeks or months is designed not only to strengthen the soldier's ability to handle mental fatigue, physical exhaustion, and emotional abuse but to integrate into the soldier's behavioral repertoire a set of skills that will become as second nature as breathing and walking. This is done for a very specific reason.

The application of learned skills becomes much more difficult under extreme emotional conditions. So, for instance, although a soldier might learn the proper technique for repairing and reloading a particular weapon, and can do this flawlessly while on base, it does not necessarily mean that he or she will do as good a job while on the field of battle, where bullets may be whizzing by one's head and one's fellow soldiers are screaming and bleeding all around the soldier's position. There is the tendency to freeze, to forget, to become overwhelmed, to get distracted. And so while learning the skill, understanding the behavioral requirements of repair and reload, or even being able to complete the task set flawlessly are *necessary*, they are not always *sufficient* in order for a recruit to be a successful soldier. For success, the soldier needs to go beyond knowing and understanding. The skill set has to become an indelible part of one's being. Something that one can do "automatically," under the most severe of conditions.

The OCD Connection

And so it is with the person with OCD. When engaged in exposure, the OCD client is like the soldier on the battlefield. Physiologically, in fact, their bodies may be behaving in very similar ways, approaching or approximating a panic attack. In both cases, knowing what to do and how to do it may not be enough in the face of this emotional and physiological upheaval. In order to be successful, for the OCD client as well as the soldier, the skills need to have been drilled to the point of becoming "second nature," so that they can be executed *in spite of* the high emotional state that the person is experiencing.

Explaining to clients with OCD how ERP works and then sending them out to do serendipitous exposure would be like giving a single lesson to soldiers on how to handle a gun, and then sending them out to do battle. And that is why, like boot camp, OCD clients need to go beyond learning by drilling via what may be termed, "structured" exposure therapy. In structured ERP, the therapy is formalized, scheduled, measured, recorded, and reported.

In structured ERP, the therapy is formalized, scheduled, measured, recorded, and reported.

In our contamination example above, a client would contract with his therapist to spend a specific period of time every day engaging in repeated exposures of touching oorknobs without washing. As an illustration, the client would contract, not only to engage in serendipitous exposure, where, over the course of the entire day each time a doorknob is encountered he will engage in some kind of ERP challenge, but also that between 12:30 and 1:00 p.m. each workday, he will walk around the building, seeking out as many doors as can be found, make the effort to touch as many of them as possible (at whatever level of touching he is at in his hierarchy), and will be aware and record the level of experienced anxiety before, during, and after the ERP exercise. For the weekends the contract might include going downtown for an hour, opening and closing the doors to the different business establishments along Main Street, and again monitoring, recording, and then reporting the levels of experienced anxiety. Alternatively, the contract might not specify how long the ERP session will take but rather specify the minimum number of doorknobs that need to be touched.

Structured exposure is not left to chance encounters, so there is more control of the learning process on the part of the client. There is more assurance that a minimum amount of time or a minimum number of exposure experiences will be accomplished each day. We know that ERP is most successful when it is repeated, prolonged, and meets a minimum level of intensity. With structured exposure, the client has much more direct control over these variables. Finally, just as boot camp better prepares the soldier to successfully utilize learned skills under the most extreme of emotional conditions, so, too, structured exposure prepares the client with OCD to better weather whatever he encounters during the emotionally heightened states that are triggered by serendipitous exposure.

Jay August's

Both my wife and I smoked cigarettes back when we were students at Rutgers University in New Jersey. There was a restaurant–bar at the time that we used to frequent named Jay August's. It was a fixture in the college town of New Brunswick with a history that went back maybe a hundred years. We would go there, socialize with friends, eat, and more than just about any place else that we spent time at, we smoked. Although smoking is no longer permitted in eating establishments in the state of New Jersey, this was not the case in the early 1980s. Jay August's was therefore our haven, our escape from the stress of graduate school, a place to kick back and relax, a place to have a good time. And smoking was a part of that experience for us.

We both quit smoking at the same time for the same reasons many of our friends were quitting: health concerns, money concerns, environmental concerns, and so on. And during those first few weeks, especially for my wife, who had been a significantly heavier smoker than I had ever been, it was a time of great stress and challenge. We had decided to quit together so that we could support each other through the process. I for one found that there were certain things that would "trigger" my urge to smoke, and, understanding that I just needed some time to "detox" from the nicotine and get adjusted to being a non-smoker, I decided that I would need to avoid certain places or activities during the early stages of quitting.

We quit in late spring, and I found out after a single visit to the Jersey shore that being at the beach in general was a very strong trigger. I found that having a cup of coffee was also a powerful trigger. In addition, barbecues unexpectedly triggered my urge to smoke. My wife, on the other hand, found that playing card games, watching TV, and eating spicy foods made her feel more like having a cigarette. And so, during the spring and summer of that year, we avoided most of these places and activities and creatively engaged in alternative forms of entertainment, such as bicycling and going to the movies.

The list of triggers enumerated above was found out mostly by trial and error. We did not know in advance exactly what would make us feel like engaging in smoking and only discovered our personal triggers by watching how we felt when we did certain things or went to certain places. But there was one exception to this, and that was Jay August's.

We knew without visiting the place that Jay August's would be a significant challenge for both of us. The sights, sounds, smells, and emotions associated with that place would most definitely catapult us into a nicotine fit, we assumed, and so in an effort to make the quitting process as pain-free as possible, we opted to forgo visiting the restaurant for the entire summer.

When summer ended, classes resumed, and the stress of studies made us long to return to our favorite eating and drinking establishment. By early fall we had both gotten over much of the day-to-day struggle of quitting smoking, but we feared that if we were to step into Jay August's our addiction would be ignited anew. We knew there was no way around it. If we wanted to be able to frequent the restaurant, we needed to begin going there. It was time.

This was the plan. We would go together and meet some friends there who knew we were going to the restaurant for the first time as nonsmokers. We went with the understanding that if either one of us felt an uncontrollable urge to smoke, we would inform the other that we needed to leave immediately. The agreement was that, regardless of whether or not the other person felt the need to leave at that moment, we would leave together without delay. We picked a day to go, and on the way there we talked about what this visit really meant and defined our purpose and intent.

We were not going to Jay August's to have a good time. We were not going to enjoy the food and the social atmosphere. We were going for one reason and one reason only: We were going in order to experience being in Jay August's without having a cigarette. We might feel uncomfortable, anxious, even frustrated. Distracted by other smokers at the bar, we might have difficulty concentrating on the conversation. We might find ourselves not enjoying the food very much because of mental anguish. But no matter, the point was to *be* there without a cigarette in our mouths.

We fully expected that, just like barbecues and card games, we would eventually get to the point that we could engage in this activity as well, without cigarettes, and be able to enjoy ourselves. But that was not going to happen today. Today was just about going through the experience. We accepted that if we wanted to reach our goal of being able to use this facility as a place to destress, then we would need to recondition our responses to being there, and that would mean going through a period where we would not be particularly comfortable. We knew this would be difficult, but it would be temporary, and there would be a payoff.

As it turned out, we didn't need to leave, even the first time, but we were moderately uncomfortable. By the second time it was already much better, and soon we were "free"

We knew this would be difficult, but it would be temporary, and there would be a payoff.

to visit Jay August's and reenergize ourselves with friends, food, and good times once again.

The OCD Connection

In session, you can apply this story or one like it whenever a client complains that engaging in ERP, while doable, will interfere with his functioning, either at work, school, or at play. As an illustration, I once shared this story in session with a 16-year-old client with OCD who had an "evenness" obsession that resulted in subtle behavioral compulsions involving slight ritualized movements in her fingers. She found that these compulsive movements were becoming more elaborate over time, and although she was able to engage in them without being noticed, she was beginning to worry that her friends would become more aware of what she was doing and start asking questions.

She came to me in distress about her condition but also with much reservation about treatment. She told me that she was afraid to engage in the treatment, even though she freely admitted that she did not really think that anything "horribly dangerous" would happen if she stopped herself from compulsively moving her fingers. She confessed to me, in fact, that she expected, not only based on what I had told her but based on her own research, that through the process of habituation, any uncomfortable feelings resulting from exposure therapy would quickly fade away. Her concern was, to use her own words, "For however long it *does* take, I won't be able to function if I don't do those finger movements! I won't be relaxed with my friends, and I won't be able to have fun!"

She was right, of course. If she stopped her ritualizing, she should expect that she would feel a certain degree of discomfort, anxiety, and preoccupation, and that this would result in her being less spontaneous with her friends. My goal in working with her was to help her redefine her own expectations about having fun with her friends. "If you want to get over your OCD," I told her, "then for the first few times that you get together with your friends while committing yourself to not engage in your finger ritual, you should *expect* that you won't have a particularly good time. You are not, in fact getting together with them to *have* a good time. Rather, you are getting together with them to see what it feels like to spend time without ritualizing. That is the point of the exercise. The fun will come back at a later time, but for now, expect *not* to have fun, just as my wife and I anticipated at Jay August's."

By redefining the goal as one of just getting through an experience while not engaging in ritualizing, I addressed her perfectionistic thinking and consequent expectations that she should be able to fully enjoy herself, even as she was first challenging her OCD behaviors. This was unrealistic. While emphasizing the temporary nature of the discomfort and the attainable goal of being able to be with her friends and have fun without engaging in any ritual behaviors, I encouraged her to "bite the bullet" and forgo a little fun now for the sake of freedom, control, power, and victory over her OCD.

On Becoming an Athlete

Let's consider two adolescent boys, Jordan and Devin. Both are fourteen, high school freshman, do well in class, and have a good circle of friends. They are both the same height and weight, and both are roughly in the same physical shape. Jordan is an avid team sports player. He has played basketball and baseball since he was in grade school, started playing volleyball in middle school, and is presently on the high school football team. Devin, on the other hand, hikes and bicycles but has never played organized team sports of any kind.

Let's say we take the two boys, both of whom have never played a game of soccer, and begin to instruct them in the game. We soon have them join teams and play competitively against other teams. Which of the two boys, all else being equal, will catch on more quickly to the game of soccer and will do better as a player in the team games?

Although there is no guarantee of this, the logical conclusion would be to bet on Jordan. Why? Because Jordan has been trained in team sports, Devin hasn't. Even though Jordan has never played soccer, he has lots of experience getting a sense of his body relative to a ball and having a sense of his space relative to other team players. Psychologists would say that his athletic skills would be more readily able to "generalize" to soccer compared to Devin's, who, while athletic in his own way, has less experience with teams and with team ball playing.

The OCD Connection

Sometimes at the start of therapy, when OCD clients learn about exposure and response prevention, they become disheartened.

They say, "There are *so* many symptoms that I have, even if ERP works, it will take me forever to get to a normal level of functioning!" Even if the symptom presentation is limited to one area of OCD, say, contamination obsessions with washing compulsions, the client may feel that so many things in daily life are contaminated that significant recovery seems very far away. But to assume this would be a mistake. As a therapist, you can employ the above discussion about Jordan and Devin to demonstrate to the client why this is so.

In practice, application of ERP skills to a client's compulsive behavior may be very difficult and stressful at first, but very often, as the person applies ERP to challenge more of her compulsions, the recovery rate and the length of time of discomfort tend to decrease. For instance, let's assume that the levels of perceived contamination of the furniture in a living room are all equal, so that on a scale of 1–10, the sofa is a 5, as are the recliner, the coffee table, and the floor lamp.

If the client touches the sofa, and then goes and "spreads" that contamination to another (less contaminated) section of the house repeatedly over a period of time, she will find that her anxiety level will drop down, and that the 5 eventually becomes a 2 or less. If she then touches the recliner, and spreads the contamination by touching another section of the house, and goes on later to do the same with the coffee table, she will find that when she goes to touch the floor lamp and then spreads it to another section of the house, the contamination may not be as high as 5 this time around and that the level 2 is reached much more quickly.

This occurs as a result of generalization. Even though the person is touching the lamp for the first time in the exposure exercise and is spreading it to an as yet uncontaminated section of the house, ERP will be less painful and will be negotiated more quickly, because the person is becoming desensitized not only to the individual items that are being touched but also to the whole process of ERP.

One would expect this to happen because, as the client employs ERP more frequently to various contaminated items, she is learning through her experience that the initial anxiety wanes after a period of repeated exposure. It thus becomes easier to trust that the anxiety generated by the next thing that is touched will also lessen over time. This expectation, the trust that the fear response to touching the next contaminated object will soon dissipate, helps the client to "move through" the fear more quickly.

If done properly, ERP is always a challenge. However, as a the client becomes experienced using ERP to successfully challenge and control OCD symptoms, trust in the technique builds, and it becomes less difficult and requires less time to challenge the next set of symptoms. As with Jordan, there is a sense of competence that transfers to different, but similar, situations.

There is a sense of competence that transfers to different, but similar situations.

Force of Habit

If you are an adult and you wear contacts, chances are that you wore glasses for a while before you changed over. If this is the case, you might have had a similar experience to the one I am about to describe. When you first got your contacts, even before you were fully used to them, you immediately realized several advantages in addition to the obvious change in your appearance. For example, the first time you walked in the rain, you were able to keep your head up and feel the drops on your face, not needing to worry about getting your glasses all spotty. You realized the freedom of being able to walk into a warm building on a very cold day and not need to worry about your lenses fogging all up. Perhaps you enjoyed the fact that you could now swim and ski without the discomfort and awkwardness of glasses or risking the dangers of not wearing them during those activities.

But you might have also become aware of something completely unexpected. Over the years you might have developed certain habits around wearing your glasses. For instance, imagine that you are wearing your new contact lenses, and you drop a book as you are walking. You bend down to pick it up, and as you return to your fully upright standing position, you take your index finger and push up against the bridge of your nose. It is as if you are pushing back into place your eyeglasses that would have slipped forward a bit when you bent down, had you been wearing them. Although you find yourself somewhat amused at this interesting little habit that you had developed and were never even aware of, you are surprised at how many times in the following weeks, even months, you find yourself engaging in that same behavior whenever you move or bend in some fashion that would have dislodged your glasses a bit had you been wearing them.

This is a habit. A habit that has become completely natural to you after many years of repetition. Although it required a deliberate and keenly timed arm movement, you did it without any effort and, indeed, found that it persisted even after you had made a conscious attempt to stop doing it. This is the power of repetition when it comes to habit development.

The OCD Connection

In therapy your OCD clients will usually get to a point where they learn how to use ERP treatment successfully resulting in better control over a symptom or two. Many clients, however, present with a long and varied list of symptoms, symptoms which dictate how and when they should do or not do many things over the course of each day. These clients will complain, saying "Sure, I see how to use ERP successfully, but it was a lot of hard work, and sometimes very anxiety-provoking! I have *so many* different rituals and obsessions—it will take me forever to get a handle on all of them, and will produce more anxiety than I think I can handle!"

Although this response is understandable, these sentiments do not necessarily reflect the way things actually work. Usually, without treatment, OC symptoms often spread from one thing to another, creating new obsessions or rituals, or extending and complicating older ones. Likewise, in treatment, the recovery from symptoms (usually in the form of better control as opposed to complete elimination of symptoms) spread from one situation to another. With a few successes under one's belt, most OCD clients find that applying ERP to additional symptoms doesn't take as long and requires less effort than when they first tackled the original symptoms.

OCD clients find that applying ERP to additional symptoms doesn't take as long and requires less effort than when they first tackled the original symptoms.

Some such clients even get to the point where they "automatically" engage in ERP interventions whenever a symptom emerges, much in the same way that one can push up against eyeglasses that are no longer there. Repetition of ERP techniques makes them an integrated part of the client's repertoire of behaviors. They can become automatic responses to OC symptoms, taking only a small fraction of the effort needed to combat those symptoms first attacked at the start of treatment. They become, in essence, a new habit, although one that the client, with your help, created on purpose and one that works for *him* rather than for the OCD. Combating all those lists of daily symptoms therefore becomes much less of an overwhelming task than one might assume based on the ERP experiences earlier in treatment. As is usually the case with the behavioral treatment of OCD, the therapeutic advice remains, "Stick with it—it will get less difficult with time."

Mind Games in the Shower

As many of my friends and family members (especially my wife) will tell you, I am often forgetful. This tends to manifest itself as little annoyances on a daily basis. For example, I will often misplace my pen several times over the course of a day, or I might forget why I walked into a room.

On one occasion, I was supposed to pick up a good friend of mine in New York City on my way traveling through from Long Island to New Jersey. I drove right through the city, completely oblivious to the arrangements that we had reviewed only the night before, leaving her standing on a street corner in midtown Manhattan for several hours. As this was the time before the ubiquitous presence of cell phones, I did not even find out about this error until later that night when that same friend phoned me at home. When she realized that I was still not aware of my negligence from earlier in the day, she proceeded to ask how I was doing and engaged me in conversation for a full five minutes, just to see how long it would take me to remember. When it finally dawned on me that I had in fact forgotten to pick her up earlier that day, I was horrified and apologetic.

I have tried using such interventions as relaxation techniques or mindfulness meditation to help me maintain better focus, but the helpfulness of these efforts are only as effective as how often one remembers to practice them or use them: I often forget to do both!

Curiously, I have found that during down-time, periods where I am not actively involved in a particular task that requires a lot of concentration, thoughts of things that I need to remember tend to pop up. For instance, while I am lying in bed, just before falling asleep, I will often remember something that I have to do the next day, or something I should have done earlier during the day just ending. When possible, I take advantage of these moments of revelation and will jump out of bed to take care of the situation or write myself a reminder for the next day with the paper and pen I keep next to my bed.

Sometimes, however, I have these flashes of memory under less favorable conditions. During my morning shower is a good example. You would think that if I remember something during my shower that I would at least remember it long enough to write it down someplace when I exited the shower. No such luck.

Once, I wanted to bring a book from my home to my office. I remembered this in the midst of my morning shower and completely forgot about it by the time I was dressed. A couple of days later, this happened again, and so while standing in the shower I mentally repeated, "Do not forget to bring the textbook into the office with you today!" By the time I was towel drying, the memory was gone.

Several days later, it happened yet again. This time I was really determined to remember that book! I recalled a memory trick I had once learned. If I could connect the thought of bringing the book to work with something outside of the shower, maybe that thing would trigger the thought of the book. So I thought to myself, "Don't forget to bring the book with you to the office!" and as I did so, I also visualized my hand grabbing hold of the doorknob of the door exiting from my house. I repeated this visualization and mental statement several times.

In one of those very rare "Oh my!" experiences that we have only once in a very great while, I did end up forgetting about the book once again upon exiting the shower, and a bit later, as I turned the doorknob to leave my house, the memory flashed back through my mind, loud and clear. "Don't forget to bring the book to the office!" I couldn't believe it! My time in the shower repeatedly reviewing the visual image of my turning the doorknob together with the thought to remember the book had somehow connected the two. I have found that this technique is not infallible, but I do use it regularly, and find that, at least for me, there is about a 40 percent hit rate for success.

When two different things occur simultaneously, or immediately one after another over and over again, they become linked somehow in our minds.

Why does the technique work at all? It works because of the process of creating an association. Behaviorally speaking, when two different things occur simultaneously, or immediately one after another over and over again, they become linked somehow in our minds. Ivan Pavlov, the famous Russian experimenter, introduced us to the idea of classical conditioning. It was by pairing the sound of a bell with the delivery of food that an association was created between the two. Dogs in this experiment ultimately salivated in response to the sound of the bell ringing alone, because that sound and the experience of food delivery had become paired, since one always followed the other. It was this association between the bell and food delivery that had allowed the process of classical conditioning to take place.

Similarly, when I was listening to the radio in my car not too long ago, a song came on that I had not heard for a very long time. I immediately got a very nostalgic feeling, a sense of closeness and comfort that was quite strong. About three seconds later, I remembered that this song was the one that I had listened to repeatedly many, many times over a particular summer when I was fifteen years old. It was a great summer, and I had made a lot of new friends.

What was interesting about the radio experience was that I got those strong nostalgic feelings *before* I even remembered that the song had those memories connected with it. An association had been created between the song and my experience that summer so long ago, an association so strong, that the song itself triggered an emotional reaction in me that would normally have come in response to the memory of that summer, just as Pavlov's dogs responded with salivation to the bell, as if it were the food itself being placed before them.

The OCD Connection

You can help your clients to use this tool of creating an association on purpose to better challenge their OCD obsessions. Here is how: Most OCD clients have a strong avoidance reaction both to those things or activities that trigger their obsessions and the resulting anxiety. They either avoid them entirely or, if this becomes difficult or impossible, will immediately react to their obsession-produced discomfort with some attempt at neutralizing their anxiety, usually by engaging in some kind of ritualistic behavior. But they can instead choose to apply the concept of creating an association in this situation, better enabling themselves to actively fight their OCD symptoms rather than succumbing to them.

Allow me to illustrate. A client of mine, whom I shall call Stevie, would quickly react to anything that was even slightly out of place by moving the object carefully until it was in its "correct" position. When the item was in the "wrong" place, as it was experienced by Stevie, it created a sense of emotional discomfort or even intense anxiety. As is natural and logical, Stevie's automatic response to this situation was to reduce this level of discomfort by engaging in the ritual of fiddling with the object until it was in a position that no longer created discomfort. Seeing an object out of place was therefore linked to having such thoughts as, "I must do something to make this discomfort go away," which logically lead to the resulting ritualistic behavior. But what if Stevie could change the link between this set of circumstances and his own thoughts?

What if this client learned to see each obsession and its resulting anxiety as an opportunity *to apply his skills of exposure and response prevention?*

What if this client learned to see each obsession and its resulting anxiety as an *opportunity* to apply his skills of exposure and response prevention? What if each time his OCD symptoms are triggered, he can experience it not as a signal to work at lowering his anxiety in the short term by ritualizing, but as a chance to fight back against his disorder, and ultimately attain better control over it, in the long term? By implementing such a strategy, he has essentially reconditioned himself so as to more easily (and more enthusiastically) remember to engage in his ERP strategies.

If each time this client sees something "out of place" he now practices rewriting his internal dialogue to read something like, "Here is a great opportunity to fight back against my OCD and gain some ground in my attempt to get better control over it!" then eventually the thoughts of avoiding, escaping, or neutralizing his discomfort by engaging in some ritual fade into the background. Instead, each time he feels anxiety in response to an obsessive trigger, he automatically gets motivated to use this opportunity to his advantage—and engage in ERP.

Just as reviewing the image of grabbing the doorknob and linking it with the thought of bringing the book to the office resulted in the real doorknob triggering this memory, so, too, obsessive-driven anxiety can be linked to thoughts of using ERP. Through a story such as this one, you can help your clients learn that under exposure conditions, anxiety need no longer be a signal to avoid, escape, or neutralize but, rather, a signal to aggressively attack the OCD by refusing to "do as it says" and a signal to worsen the obsession on purpose while "watching the OCD with one's third eye," as if to say "Not *this* time!"

Cutting Toenails

If you are or have ever been the parent of a young child, you are probably familiar with the ritual of cutting your child's toenails once every couple of weeks or so. Bernice is a young mother, and on one occasion, she had the mild misfortune of cutting her daughter Kelly's toenail a little too close to the skin, breaking it ever so slightly, so that there was the tiniest hint of blood visible at the skin line. Five-year-old Kelly responded, like most children her age would have, with a combination of intense anger and hysterical fear. This was intensified by the fact that on this particular occasion Kelly actually saw the blood herself, though the injury practically required a microscope to identify the bleeding. After attempting to calm her down, Bernice gave up for the evening, and knew that her daughter would be very resistant in the future to further toenail cutting.

When enough time had passed, Bernice got around to addressing Kelly's growing toenails once again. She was, as expected, extremely anxious and resistant to Mom's approach with the nail clippers. Kelly ultimately complied, but would yell at her mother if she felt Mom was cutting her nails too close to the skin, and would flinch constantly as Mom continued clipping her nails, even when Mom wasn't anywhere near touching her skin with the clippers.

Kelly was on guard because she felt out of control. Somebody was doing something to her that could result in pain and discomfort if done incorrectly, and this gave her the feeling of vulnerability. Once she had already experienced the pain of having a toenail cut too short she became extremely hypervigilant, always watching very carefully what Mom did with a sense of heightened anxiety, and always anticipating the possibility of another error in judgment and the potentiality for pain.

Bernice did not force the issue, and after several weeks of this struggle, she decided to hand the clippers over to her daughter. Under her watchful guidance at first, Kelly began to cut her nails by herself. Because she was now controlling the speed of the cutting and the specific parts of the nails that were being cut, she became more relaxed and was able to cut them closer to the skin.

When people are anxious about doing something, when they struggle with confronting a fear, if another person attempts to force them to confront that fear, it usually results in an escalation of the fear, and, when possible, the "digging in of their heels." They will resist or even refuse, sometimes even rebel by arguing or fighting back in some way. Pushing harder will often result in even greater rebellion. This happens because dealing with a fear engenders a sense of not being in control. When it is dictated to you that you *must* confront that fear, those feelings of not being in control become even greater, resulting in even greater levels of the fear, and ultimately greater resistance to confronting it. The final result is behavioral paralysis—avoidance of the feared object or behavior and the suspension of the process of conquering the fear.

The OCD Connection

The above story can be used in explaining to family members why you are handing the control of treatment to the client, even if she is a child. You can explain that in the treatment of OCD, it is best if the speed and direction of the treatment are determined by the client, and not the therapist or a family member for the reasons illustrated in the story.

In the treatment of OCD, it is best if the speed and direction of the treatment are determined by the client.

When you first introduce the concept of exposure treatment to your client in therapy, you should explain the nature of the therapeutic relationship. "We are driving in the car together, you and I," you might say. "You are in the driver's seat, with your hands on the steering wheel and your feet on the gas and the brake pedals. I'm just the person in the passenger seat holding the directions and the map." Of course, keeping with the latest developments in technology, you might identify yourself as the GPS system in the car.

The main point of the metaphor is to communicate to your client that she is in control of the speed and direction of treatment. In so doing, you hope to help allay any concerns that she may have about being "forced" to confront her fears. This strategy usually results in the client paradoxically confronting her fears faster and to a more intense degree than she would have had you put undo pressure on her to do so. Just like the small child cutting her own toenails, feeling in control of the process of confronting one's fears allows one to move forward more quickly with greater confidence and courage.

Spelunking

When I was in graduate school, I worked as a mental health aide at an inpatient psychiatric hospital. Together with several dozen other "twenty-somethings," I worked at different units in the hospital and across three different time shifts. Being around the same age and having the same interests (most of us were in school for psychology or clinical social work), we would also tend to socialize outside of work. On one occasion, a whole bunch of us went camping and hiking together for a weekend. There were about twenty-two of us, mostly mental health aides, but there were a few psychiatric nurses and psychiatrists who came along.

Unbeknownst to the rest of us, the two people who had planned the trip worked it out so that we would be camping near an old cave, and the plan was for us to all go cave exploring or "spelunking." Spelunking is not about entering into those caves that are fully lit with electric lights and have steps built into them. It does not refer to those caves that have walkways and tour guides and protective barriers. Spelunking is about putting on a hard hat with a light on it, strapping yourself to a rope, and being lowered into a deep hole where you then find yourself walking, squeezing yourself through, and sometimes even crawling on your belly through narrow passages in complete and utter darkness. The air is thick, still, and humid. Sharp shards of rock stick out from everywhere waiting to cut into your leg or shoulder. The ground is littered with stones of all shapes and sizes, just waiting to grab your ankle and twist it.

This was not my idea of fun, but it was sprung on all of us by surprise once we were already at the campsite, and the peer pressure to not "chicken out" was intense. We all got up in the morning, went to the local equipment rental place, and began our adventure. Once we all got down into the cave entrance and we started to walk deeper into the cave, it became clear that many, if not all of us, were very nervous.

And then it started. Someone started joking about how, if you are going to get a major panic attack, what better place than when you are surrounded by twenty-one other mental health professionals? And then there was talk of the intense embarrassment of "losing it" in front of all these professionals with whom you work, and having to then see everyone the next day when we would be back at work at the hospital. Everyone laughed. A lot. In fact, we laughed about a lot of things. I cannot remember the specific lines that people were throwing out as we made our way through the cave passageways, but everything seemed funny. Absolutely everything. I remember thinking that I could not remember ever having laughed so hard and for so long.

In retrospect, although many of the people I worked with were truly funny, clever people, I expect that things seemed funnier than they normally would because we were all so terrified down there. Humor and laughter help tremendously to ward off any real feelings of panic. It seemed to me, in thinking about it afterwards, that laughter and terror were to some degree mutually exclusive experiences; when you feel one strongly, it is very hard to feel the other. Also, it seemed that in specifically making fun of ourselves, in this case our own anxiety about being down in the cave, we provided for ourselves a kind of wider perspective, and objectivity, a distance from the anxiety that served to ground us.

Humor and laughter help tremendously to ward off any real feelings of panic.

The OCD Connection

There has been much written in OCD books supporting the use of humor in treatment. I have heard on more than one occasion a presenter on the topic of OCD stating that when a client has a good sense of humor, it is a prognostic indicator for treatment success. When I first joined the Obsessive Compulsive Foundation, I remember receiving, among other things in the mail, a few buttons with humorous statements printed on them. "OCF: Every Member Counts," was one of them. I remember having a very positive reaction to those buttons. It seemed like a very healthy thing to do, to poke fun at oneself in this way. Not in a self-disparaging way, mind you, as you can make fun of yourself without necessarily putting yourself down.

Not everybody is in the same place when it comes to the use of humor. Some are too overcome by their comorbid depression, and others are just more serious by nature. Still others just aren't quite ready yet, as they try to cope with understanding the nature of their disorder, how it affects them, and how to fight back. But in general, most people find it therapeutic to see the humor in their situation, and they appreciate the opportunity to laugh with others about the bizarre quality of their lives with OCD. In therapy, feel free to introduce humor into your sessions, even with your most debilitated clients. Through stories such as the one above, you can illustrate concretely how humor can be an effective way of dealing with high levels of stress. Humor can therefore be an important tool in your clients' toolbox of skills designed to negotiate OCD through the application of ERP.

Chocolate Cake

Ethan, a four-year-old, comes into the kitchen, and sees his mom frosting a chocolate cake she had baked earlier in the day. He asks if he can have some, and Mom says he may not, as the cake is for Daddy's birthday celebration later that night, after dinner.

Ethan insists, "But I want it *now*!"

"You will ruin Daddy's surprise if I cut you a piece, and you will also ruin your appetite for dinner," Mom calmly retorts. Ethan insists Daddy won't mind if there is just one piece missing from the cake, offers to pass on having a piece later if he could have one now, and promises he will eat all his dinner later and that the cake won't spoil his appetite. Mom stands firm, offers him a small snack of a couple of crackers instead of the cake, but Ethan is not interested and storms out of the kitchen.

A bit later, Mom is in the basement looking for some party decorations, and Ethan sees his opportunity to get what he wants. He walks quietly into the kitchen, climbs up on a chair that he has positioned next to the countertop where the cake is sitting, and removes the plastic cover from the cake holder. He takes his hand, grabs a fistful of chocolate cake, and is about to take his first delicious bite when Mom, who has returned from the basement, yells from the other side of the kitchen, "Put that cake down!"

Ethan is startled in response to this surprise, but he recovers in a matter of seconds. A frown forms on his face and with a scowl at his mother he shouts back, "NO! I won't!"

"You put that cake down right now, young man, or you will go right to bed for the rest of the night!" comes the parental response.

Exasperated and frustrated with the lack of power over his life, Ethan screams, "Fine!" and throws the cake in his hand down on the floor. He did as he was told, but with a twinkle in his eye, and just a touch of smirk on his face, he essentially communicates to Mom, "Gotcha! I might have done what you demanded of me, but I did it *my* way, so that you really didn't get what you wanted in the way that you wanted it!"

When one is being told what to do and wants to refuse to cooperate, but is not in a position of power to do so, one can choose to comply in a way that communicates to the one in power that he, the less powerful, can still exercise some degree of control over the situation. Because the person is being compliant, but at the same time is, in some way, being passive-aggressive, we might call this kind of response, *passive-aggressive compliance*. It is a "Yes, Sir!" response with a "Go jump in a lake! I don't have to listen to you!" as a subtitle.

The OCD Connection

When challenging OCD within the context of an ERP exercise, there are times when the OCD client does not feel capable of fighting the OCD voice in his head and refraining completely from engaging in the compulsive ritual. Say, after touching a contaminated object, the person feels compelled to wash his hands and does not feel capable of putting off this activity for even a short period of time. He feels powerless against the OCD, acquiesces, and prepares himself to engage in the ritual as dictated by his disorder.

But as the therapist you have at your disposal a technique that you can share with your client, which is represented in the story above. Your message to your client is essentially, "OK, so you can't postpone engaging in this ritual, and you don't feel that you can refrain from washing your hands, but what *can* you do? How *can* you fight back?" The challenge here is for the client to allow himself to comply with the demands of the OCD but to do so in a way that allows for the demonstration of some vestige of self-determination on the part of the client. The possibilities are infinite, and the client can choose from a myriad of ways to exercise greater control over the situation. He can turn the faucet on and pump the soap with the hand that does not usually initiate those behaviors. He can use no soap or pump the dispenser a fewer number of times than he usually does. He can wash in the kitchen sink instead of the bathroom. He can wash the hand he usually washes first, second. If he has to rub his fingers up and down, one at a time, from the thumb to the pinky, he can do it in reverse order, or skip a finger. He can choose to leave one square inch of the back of one of his hands as "unscrubbed." Or he could do a combination of several of these.

In this way the client is essentially saying to the OCD, "Fine! You win! I will wash my hands as you say, but I will do it on *my* terms, in *my* way!" By doing this, he begins to break down the habitual nature of the particular sequence of behaviors, paving the way for him to be able to completely abandon it in the future. In addition, the client can redefine his relationship with his OCD, from one of mere compliance to one of passive-aggressive compliance. The "Go jump in a lake!!" nature of this attitude shift becomes the bedrock, the foundation from which he is ultimately able to engage in a complete rebellion against the OCD.

The client can redefine his relationship with his OCD, from one of mere compliance to one of passive-aggressive compliance.

Someday, Ethan will become a teenager. As angry as Mom is about the chocolate cake on the floor, it may be only a prelude to what lies ahead a decade or so down the road. Good luck to you, Mom.

Snowstorms in June

When I was a graduate student I hated to study in the spring. If it was a beautiful, sunny, warm day, I had a very, very hard time getting myself to sit down and start working. I was invested in doing well in school, liked school in general, but even when I was interested in the particular subject that I was supposed to be studying, I found myself avoiding doing so. I realized early on that I needed to "externalize" my structure, that is, make changes in my environment so as to make it easier to study, and harder to avoid studying.

I came to the conclusion that my off-campus apartment had too many distractions. I could go into the fridge for a snack, take a nap, hang out in the backyard; the list of diversions was substantial. While it was easier for me to get down to working. during the winter months when the weather was warmer it was a different story. With the windows open and the warm breeze blowing, I would get distracted by the sounds coming from outside, and so I found myself making plans to leave the apartment altogether.

I made it a regular habit of going to the college library whenever I had significant studying to do. At first, I would study on the first floor in the main study area but soon found out that I would bump into people that I knew there on a regular basis, would socialize, and do very little studying. I began to study upstairs, a much quieter and less crowded part of the library, where I would relax on one of the sofas that they had available there. But even there I found myself distracted, sometimes by a person that I knew, sometimes by some of the books on the shelves, or sometimes I would nap on the sofa. Ultimately, I found that I had the greatest success when I went upstairs in the library and forced myself to sit at one of the study cubicles in the corner of the floor. I had externalized my structure, in the sense that I changed my environment so I would have fewer distractions and be less tempted to procrastinate. Also, whenever I gave into the temptation of distraction, I reevaluated my external structure plan, and made changes so that it would work more effectively. It was a trial-and-error process.

I had externalized my structure, in the sense that I changed my environment.

This worked fine until early one June, when the library was closed for a few weeks in between spring and summer semesters. I was working on my dissertation at the time, and so I was unaffected by the break in classes and still had plenty of work to do. I tried studying at home at first, but after the first four days of going for walks, bike rides, and, engaging in other diversionary behavior, I accepted that the difficulties in self-discipline that had originally prompted my library routine were still very much in effect, and I needed an alternative solution. On my way to the local public library, I had an accident with my bicycle, hurt my leg, and found it very difficult to walk. My car was in the shop, and they were waiting for a part. I found myself faced with at least two more days where I would be housebound and was committed to not wasting those days. But it was early June, and I knew that the nice weather would make following through with this commitment particularly challenging. And then I had a brainstorm.

I shut all the windows and pulled down the shades. I turned up the air conditioning so it was chilly in the apartment. I put on a sweater and made some hot cocoa. I dug through my record collection (this was the mid-1980s, and as a graduate student I could not afford the brand new technology of compact discs and the devices that played them), and found one of my old Environmental Sounds records—it was 25 minutes straight of the sounds of a winter storm—nothing more than winds howling in the distance. I put the record on, snuggled up with my text and hot cup of cocoa, and found that I soon completely forgot that it was a warm summer day in early June. Although of course at some level I knew it was not an icy cold day in mid-February, the cues in the environment that I had manipulated had a powerful effect on me, and it felt truly like midwinter. Traditionally, studying at home during the winter was less difficult for me, and so I was able to spend long hours during those two days accomplishing a good amount of work.

The OCD Connection

In the course of treatment, once OCD clients learn about their disorder and how cognitive behavioral therapy can help them, they often become extremely excited and motivated to move forward in treatment. However, very often these same clients, while poised to begin the actual implementation of learned strategies, sometimes get stuck. They almost always understand the concepts involved in exposure therapy, they report that they believe it will work, and they seem to be extremely motivated to move forward and free themselves from the emotional pain and restrictions inherent in having the disorder. Yet, they do not follow through with their homework, or what we will often call "practice" (especially with school-age clients, so as to differentiate it from the dreaded stuff they receive at school).

They come in week after week, and they say, "I just can't get myself to do this," or "I can't find the time," or a variety of similar responses. Experience in working with OCD clients has shown that what allows most of the rest of us to have a natural sense of time regarding the accomplishment of activities doesn't work that well with people who have OCD. They often struggle with how long to do something or when it's okay to stop. They can't seem to tell when something is clean enough, when something is safe enough, when something is "good enough." Because of this, doing many of the things that are quick and easy for most of us become a major chore and something to be avoided, postponed, or procrastinated. It is for this reason, for example, that people with washing compulsions will sometimes come into session having not showered for a very long time. If every time you took a shower you got "stuck" in there for four hours, how often would *you* want to take one? This results in avoidance as a coping mechanism, but of course this is not a very functional solution, and it creates a whole host of problems in living. And so, what is required for these people is a methodology to help them get started on whatever it is they need to be doing but are not doing.

Like those of us who want and know that we need to start an exercise program or make a permanent change in our diets, yet watch ourselves not doing so week after week, month after month, year after year, people with OCD need help in getting themselves to make changes in their behaviors. What is needed is the development and strengthening of what I have termed "an external sense of structure." Because really,

really wanting something doesn't always result in doing something to get it. New tools and ideas need to be introduced to help people move beyond the "stuckness." An external sense of structure provides a methodology wherein a person who has difficulty getting himself to do something manipulates his environment so as to increase the likelihood that he will do the avoided task.

Snowstorms in June illustrates the idea that the ways in which one can externalize structure are limited only by how creative one can be. The therapist can tell the story above to clients, or his or her own version of it, in order to show how externalizing structure operates within a non-OCD situation and to demonstrate the need to continuously reevaluate and change the variables manipulated in order to achieve continued success. It is then just a matter of applying these principles to the specific conditions that the client presents in therapy.

An external sense of structure provides a methodology wherein a person who has difficulty getting himself to do something manipulates his environment so as to increase the likelihood that he will do the avoided task.

For instance, with OCD clients, I typically contract with them to voicemail or e-mail me daily in order to report that they have engaged in their prescheduled exposure exercises, creating a greater sense of immediate accountability for them. Other times, clients will make doing something they like or buying something they want dependent on whether or not they first engage in their exposure work, sometimes getting a support person to withhold their reward until their practice is done. At other times they leave themselves notes in specific places as reminders to help prompt the exposure work. They use alarms to remind them to start or to time their exposure experiences. They contract with family members so that the family member agrees to work on something challenging for himself, such as going to the gym, and the person with OCD commits to working on exposure practice, and they check in with each other at the end of the day.

The list of possibilities is endless. Because variables change, as they did with my graduate studying story, one has to be vigilant, constantly reevaluating and reinventing the ways in which one externalizes structure, in order for success to continue. Externalizing structure is not a guarantee that one will be able to successfully do exposure work on a regular basis, but it can add to the probability of success.

4

Thinking Processes Associated with Exposure Therapy

Previous chapters introduced and defined exposure and response prevention (ERP) and then reviewed some of the building blocks of how the intervention operates at the behavioral level. This chapter presents stories that can be used in treatment to reinforce ideas about what clients should be *thinking* when they engage in ERP work. Some stories address how one should be thinking about one's relationship with OCD, and other stories look at how experiences with exposure itself can result in changes in one's thinking about oneself and the disorder. There is also much written here that addresses the thought processes that can interfere with successful implementation of OCD treatment and the changes in thinking that the client has to work on in order to successfully implement a behavioral program.

"I Think; Therefore I Am"

Most of us are familiar with the famous words of Descartes and perhaps even have known them since we were very young, but have we ever thought about what that philosophical statement really means? For most of us, unless we have been exposed to some kind of formal instruction in philosophy, either in a college course or by independent reading, the answer is "No."

So, for the benefit of those who may not fall into one of the above-stated categories, let's take a crash course on the meaning of this expression. Quite simply, the expression states that, as conscious entities, we know that we exist because we have an awareness of our existence. We think; therefore, this awareness—the fact that we are sentient beings—means that in some way, shape, or form, we exist. However, and this is the main point of the philosophical argument, that is *all* we know.

The argument states that, aside from the fact that we do in fact exist, there is nothing else in our entire experience of the world and ourselves that we can be truly sure of. You cannot be sure that anything else in the world exists in the way that you have come to assume it exists, or even that it exists at all. This may seem at first glance to be a ridiculous assertion, but let's stick with it and see where it takes us.

Aside from the fact that we do in fact exist, there is nothing else in our entire experience of the world and ourselves that we can be truly sure of.

Suppose you enter a small Midwestern town and come upon a hill at one end of the main street. On the side of the hill, clearly visible to anyone first entering the town, is the word "WELCOME" marked out by a series of stones, apparently painted in bright white paint. You might argue that, although you could not know for sure who put the stones there, you could be certain that *somebody* placed those stones in that particular configuration in order to welcome people (English-speaking people at that) to the town. That assertion might seem self-evident, and it would therefore contradict our philosophical statement that we know of nothing for certain except for the fact that we exist.

The philosophical argument, however, would state that, though highly unlikely, it is theoretically possible that a set of naturally bright white stones had, by forces of nature, been transported to this hillside, and ended up, quite accidentally, to form the letters that spelled out the word "WELCOME." Like the "man-in-the-moon" lunar configurations, or the constellations, like the canals on Mars or even the windswept tunnels in Utah, there are many natural occurrences that seem to have been designed by a sentient, thinking designer. And, although it was highly unlikely that this was the case with the WELCOME stones, it was still, in fact, a theoretical possibility.

"Well, we at least know that we are human beings!" might be another challenge to this philosophy. But even here we cannot be certain. What of the unlikely scenario that perhaps you are really quite a different-looking alien from another galaxy and that in fact you are in the middle of a long, long dream that started from your earliest memory and is continuing to this very moment in time, wherein you dream that you are a human being growing up on a planet called "Earth." You may wake up in a day or two, or maybe seventy years from now, and the dream will be over. You will realize at that time that everything you thought to exist, from your parents to your children, from your body to your country, indeed the entire planet itself, was only part of a very long and intricate dream, a dream that you are continuing to dream at this very moment. The only thing that does actually exist is *you*, only not as a human being but as the alien who dreamed up the human being and the life that went with it. The only constant in the overall reality of things is that in some way, you are "aware." You are a sentient, observing, thinking being.

Now, this scenario is of course highly improbable, but yet it still exists as a possibility, however unlikely. We can be *pretty sure* that the alien from another galaxy scenario is not true, but the central point of this philosophical exercise is that we really cannot be *completely sure*. It is this possibility that allows the original philosophical hypothesis to maintain that the only thing one can really be sure of, *completely* sure of, is the fact that one exists as some conscious entity, somewhere. Nothing else can be said for certain.

The OCD Connection

No idea, no concept, no truism, can be more important than this one when understanding, treating, and struggling with the problem of obsessive compulsive disorder. It is this concept that goes to the heart of the cognitive aspects of combating this mental illness.

Take the case of a young woman—we'll call her Shelly—who had the misfortune of having both anorexia nervosa and OCD. The two disorders were intertwined in many aspects, yet the OCD manifested itself in a myriad of ways such that it allowed her to qualify for both diagnoses. One of the symptoms that seemed to span across both problems was Shelley's need to go through the recycling bin at home for hours on end, checking to make sure that the labels on the discarded containers indicated that she did in fact eat what she thought she ate. She would study the nutritional contents of each container, trying to convince herself that she did in fact consume what she had intended, and not something else by accident.

When out eating in restaurants, Shelly would experience multiple obsessions doubting her own perceptions. For example, she would order a diet soda, stressing the word "diet" several times to the server and again checking with the server on delivery of the soda that it was indeed a diet drink. Often, at least in the beginning of treatment, she would then taste the soda, express doubt that maybe there was an error and that the soda was not in fact a diet soda, and would express a desire to call over the server to check again, or to maybe have the drink replaced.

Any competent behavioral therapist would avoid the trap of trying to reassure Shelly that the drink was in fact a diet one but instead would challenge her to "fly into the darkness" and move forward without being sure whether it was a diet drink or not. She might respond with statements like, "But I need to know! I have the right to know! It's not fair that I shouldn't know!"

And so, this became the focus of much of her treatment: the acceptance of "not knowing." This meant the understanding that at the heart of all OCD, whatever its manifestation, is the awful feeling that one is missing a piece of information and that, *if only* one could get that information, one would then be "OK." Is it clean enough? Is it safe enough? Am I sure that I am not gay? Is the door closed all the way? Is the item placed where it needs to be, and in just the right position? What if later I need that item that I am considering throwing away? Did I forget something? Might I be in danger? Did I hit that person with my car? Might I have hurt someone with my thoughts? Did I do that ritual long enough, just the right number of times, or in just the "right way?" And on and on and on.

Shelly needed to understand that she had to give up the quest of trying to know for sure that the soda was in fact a diet drink. She needed to accept the idea that she might have mistakenly consumed a food item that she did not intend to ingest. "The doubting disease," as OCD is often called, cannot be remedied by becoming less doubtful, but by accepting, even embracing, the doubt. The challenge is to recognize that the state of not being sure is an inherent part of our world.

"The doubting disease," as OCD is often called, cannot be remedied by becoming less doubtful, but by accepting, even embracing, the doubt.

"After all," you can tell your clients, "you could die tomorrow. You could die in a car crash on the way home from your therapy session today. You could choke on a piece of food, fall down the steps in your home and break your neck, slip in the tub, and crack your head open at any time." Still, most of the time, even people with OCD drive or ride in a car, take showers, take the steps, and eat food. Even in those cases where the OCD manifests itself in such a way that clients don't engage in some of these activities as a result of behavioral avoidance, they tend to engage in at least some of them. This gives us the opportunity to illustrate that OCD is arbitrary in its manifestation. That, without reason, some things trigger the "need to know," whereas others, just as potentially dangerous (and often with a higher probability of occurrence) do not.

Doubt is inescapable. You can never outrun it or outthink it. Shelly needed to know that her salvation, that her control, would come not from being sure about what she consumed, but by accepting that she could *never* be sure about what she consumed. She needed to accept that it was folly to think that she could ever reach such a point of being sure. Because, with the one exception that she does in fact exist, the "What if?" questions will plague every other situation she encounters. For this reason, "I think; therefore I am," can become a lethal weapon against OCD obsessions. "I think, and therefore I know I exist. Everything else is in doubt."

Statue on the Mantelpiece

Paul and John are neighbors. Paul is a nice guy. He minds his own business. He does things that neighbors are supposed to do. He doesn't have loud parties late into the evening. He keeps his grass nicely mowed. He paints his front porch every few years. He doesn't take out his recycling bins or garbage cans to the curb too early in the week, and he brings them in soon after pickup.

John, as things turn out, is not such a nice guy. After years of living next to each other without incident, John knocks on Paul's door one morning. He walks into Paul's house (Paul lets him in), and he goes over to the mantelpiece over the fireplace. On the mantelpiece there is statue that Paul had brought home on a trip a long time ago.

John picks up the statue and holds it up in the air over his head and says to Paul, "If you don't give me ten dollars, I'm going to take this statue, and I'm going to smash it on the floor into a hundred pieces." (Nice guy!) Well, Paul doesn't want him to smash his statue on the floor into a hundred pieces, so, confused but intimidated, Paul gives him ten dollars, and John gently puts the statue back in its place. He then leaves without a word.

The next day, he comes back and knocks on Paul's door again. Same thing happens—he comes in, holds up the statue, asks for ten dollars, and when Paul gives it to him, he puts the statue down and leaves. This goes on day after day, week after week. Paul begins to get really annoyed about this situation, and of course he is going through lots of cash fast. We won't get into why Paul doesn't call the police or why he keeps letting John into the house, or why he doesn't just punch John in the nose at the front door. Good ideas, but that's not part of the story. . . .

Time goes by, Paul gets really fed up, and he starts getting really, really angry about the situation. He says to himself, "I've had it with this. I can't stand it anymore!" He realizes that there is one thing that he can do to undermine John's behavior. Something different—something totally unexpected.

So the next day when John walks in through Paul's front door and before he can do anything, Paul runs to the mantelpiece. Paul takes that statue, and he himself smashes it into a hundred pieces on the floor. "What are you going to do you do now, big guy!" he says to John. Dejected, John walks out slowly and leaves Paul's house, and his bank account, in peace.

What has Paul done here? He's taken away John's power over him. He's pulled the rug out from underneath him. He's taken the wind out of his sails. He's undermined him. He's beaten him at his own game. Use whatever phrase you like, but Paul has dealt with the problem in a different kind of way. In a "backwards" sort of way, he has beaten his adversary at his own game.

Think, if you will, about the differences between traditional Western and traditional Eastern concepts of combat strategies. In Western society, when someone comes at you with a big closed fist, you come back with your own closed fist. This is the way we think. Alternatively, in Eastern societies (think judo or karate), the approach is very different. In these martial art forms, when someone comes at you with a closed fist and pushes his arm out toward you in an attempt to punch you, you grab his arm above the wrist, and using the energy of your opponent's punch, you flip him with it. You don't fight your opponent directly with the use of your own energy, rather you use the power of your opponent's assault to your advantage by redirecting it back against the person throwing the punch. This demonstrates a completely different way of dealing with physical conflict. By not fighting force directly with an opposing force, you do the unexpected by "thinking outside of the box."

By not fighting force directly with an opposing force, you do the unexpected by "thinking outside of the box."

The OCD Connection

Clients will come to the therapist for an initial evaluation, and when first hearing about ERP, they will often respond with something like, "I'm coming to you because I'm anxious all the time, and I get these obsessions, and they are just awful. And now you're telling me that you want me to make my obsessions worse on purpose?"

If the therapist wants these people to return for a second session, she'd better be able to explain to them the rationale for this so that they understand what this is and how it works. In the stories, The Bee Trap, The Horror Movie, and Swimming Pool, we reviewed the behavioral rationale for this approach. Here, we focus more on the cognitive aspects of the problem. Fighting OCD is about "attitude." It is about reexamining the way you think about your relationship with OCD. The Statue on the Mantelpiece addresses this issue.

In session, after reviewing the story above, the therapist can explain to the client the following: OCD is like a 3-year-old who wants to have candy at 5:30 at night before dinner and just won't accept any explanation for why this is a bad idea. You can't reason with OCD. You can't dialogue with it. And that's why when people approach the person with OCD and say something like, "Why can't you just stop?" or "How bad would it really be if you didn't do this ritual?" it provides no assistance whatsoever. Because effectively managing one's OCD is not about understanding. It's not about rational thought. It's none of that. This is not something you can talk to, but rather something you have to behaviorally do things to in order to undermine its potency. That's where your power lies. And that's why behavior therapy works the way behavior therapy works.

In ERP, the OCD is John, Paul's nasty neighbor. When a person with OCD engages in a ritual in response to an obsession, it is like Paul paying ten dollars to John. The specific ritual seems for the most part to prevent the dreaded catastrophe from happening (in our story, the destruction of the statue; with OCD, it could be anything), but it is just a matter of time before the OCD, like our neighbor, John, comes back demanding more "payment" in the form of additional rituals. Continuing to attempt to appease John only reinforces the chances of his returning. It would not be unexpected for John to even show up one day at Paul's front door, now expecting twenty dollars in order not to smash the statue, in the same way that OCD will often demand that a person perform more time-consuming and elaborate rituals in order to ward off the catastrophe.

And so what is required is thinking outside the box. Rather than giving into the demands of John or OCD, we instead create the very circumstance that John and OCD threaten us with. Once done, we have robbed our protagonist of his (or its) purpose. The statue may be broken, but we are free. Just as something terrible "might" happen, but the person who struggles with OCD breaks free from the clutches of OCD blackmail.

Eminem

For those of you who don't know, Eminem is a popular rap music star. He doesn't have OCD, but he has the right approach to fighting it, and that is what this story is about. A while back, Eminem starred in a fairly successful movie called "Eight Mile." In this movie, he plays a poor struggling rapper in a neighborhood slum. The culture of the teenage kids in this neighborhood is depicted quite interestingly in this movie.

It seems that the kids would often congregate in their clubs, actually just large rooms somewhere, where they would crowd in by the dozens. There would be a small stage set up at one end of the room. A sound system was set up on one side of the stage, where one of the local kids would spin records, usually slowing down and speeding up the revolutions of the records with his hand as he played them, creating the background music for the rap artists.

Young people would fill the place, and watch the rappers perform. The performance, however, was not so much a musical concert, as it was a sort of "musical boxing match." It seems that a rapper was deemed superior if he was better able to "diss" (shortened form of "disrespect") or "put down" his musical opponent.

So, the scene would look something like this: Two rappers would go onstage. One would rap to the other, using put downs and derogatory statements of some kind aimed at the opposing rapper. When he finished, the second rapper would then rap back to the first rapper, also putting him down as best he could. Based on the intensity of the crowd applause, it was determined who had won the interchange, and the winning rapper would then musically "mix it up" with the next challenger.

Because this was a small community of kids, they all pretty much knew each other, so that these musical put downs were not always general in nature but rather quite specific to the person being rapped to. For instance, if a girl had just broken off a relationship with one of the rappers, most everyone in the crowd would have known about it. On stage, the opposing rapper would make sure to work in this information into his rap song, suggesting perhaps that the rapper he is musically attacking was not "man enough" to "keep his woman."

The movie leads up to the ultimate rap contest between Eminem and the leading rapper in town. As he is about to go onstage, one of Eminem's friends praises him, telling him how brave he thinks Eminem is for going up onstage that night, seeing that so many things had happened lately that would give his opponent ammunition against him in this contest. (Eminem's mother, for instance, was an alcoholic and was prostituting herself, but many other negative events had occurred of which the movie observer, and the community of kids in the movie, knew about.)

In the pivotal moment of the movie, we see Eminem ascending to the stage, obviously disturbed by his friend's remarks, and thinking intensely as to how he can resolve the problem of his vulnerability. Surely his opponent knows of his personal shame and embarrassment and will capitalize on it in his rap attack. What is our hero to do?

In a flash of genius, Eminem requests to go first in this exchange. The opponent agrees to this, as it is usually seen as advantageous to go second in these matters, just as it would be desirable to have the last word in a debate. In his rap, Eminem chooses not his opponent as the target of his venomous lyrics, but to the surprise of everyone at the club, he instead chooses himself! He spends his full two minutes of allotted time hanging his own dirty laundry, one might say, but his self-denigration is done with a style communicating strength and survivorship, rather than self-loathing. The opposing rapper, now left with nothing to say, since Eminem had already beaten him to the punch, is left speechless, and simply acquiesces, leaving the stage. The crowd cheers, and our hero is triumphant.

The OCD Connection

This paradox is at the heart of the success of ERP for the treatment of OCD. If I "beat OCD to the punch" by making my obsession even worse than the OCD originally intended, I leave it with nothing to do. The story of Eminem allows the therapist to illustrate why the client is being asked to think the worst on purpose, rather than reassure himself that, in spite of engaging in ERP behavior, everything will be OK. This latter response seems to be the more logical one, after all. So properly "selling" the idea of doing "cognitive exposure," in addition to the behavioral exposure, is of paramount importance for the therapist. Once the story is told, you can then illustrate how it would be played out within the context of your client's particular presentation of OCD.

Properly "selling" the idea of doing "cognitive exposure," in addition to the behavioral exposure, is of paramount importance for the therapist.

For example, an obsession occurs to me that I hit someone with my car while I wasn't paying close attention. Rather than go back and check, or review the ride in my mind in order to reassure myself that I didn't hit anyone, I attack the OCD. I think to myself *on purpose* that, yes, indeed, I might have actually hit someone, and blood is perhaps at this very moment dripping from the grill of my car, which is parked in my garage. The stream of blood has led the police to my home, and at any moment there will be sirens wailing down my street, and it's off to jail I go!

By focusing, elaborating, and coloring in the details of my obsession, I leave the OCD with nothing more to do "to me." It is finished, as I have already done it all to myself. The OCD, no longer having any power over me, is left with nothing to do but to leave the stage, and I am triumphant!

Asking for More

When a person receives criticism, there are certain ways that she will tend to respond. One possibility is to get very quiet, say, "Okay fine," and leave the room. It is essentially a strategy based on the "escape" response—getting out of the uncomfortable situation as quickly as possible.

Other people will react to the same criticism by giving all kinds of explanations and reasons as to why they did whatever they did that got them into trouble to begin with, or with what is known as "the defensive response." Yet another typical response is to blame another person—"It wasn't me, it was Harry. Yeah, Harry did it," or what might be termed, "the deflection response." Finally, they might employ the "offensive response" strategy and counter attack—"Me!? What about you? What about what you did last time?" "You know, if you would have given me the information earlier, I would have had that report done on time," or something along those lines.

All of these responses have specific and often negative consequences. This is why in communication skills programs what is often provided is yet another, alternative strategic response. Such a response has been titled "Asking for More" in certain assertiveness training programs. In Asking for More, you present a series of questions designed to clarify for yourself why this person is upset with you, what it was exactly that you did that created this problem, and how you might avoid the problem in the future.

For example, suppose your boss is angry at you after you recently sent her a report that she had requested. You then ask her, "You are telling me that you're upset about the report. What is it about the report that was a problem?" She responds, "It was ten pages long instead of seven." "How was that a problem?" you ask. "It was a problem because my time is limited, and I need to review the report before the presentation. That is why I set the limits on the length of these reports!" she retorts. "So you are saying that the seven pages wasn't a guideline, but a requirement. I had a lot of information that I thought was very important and wasn't sure how to put all that information into the seven pages that you asked for. What would you have had me leave out?" is your next question. After she clarifies these details, you then say, "Well, okay, so you're telling me that if I would have left out these pieces of information and I would have gotten the report to you a little bit earlier so that you could have reviewed it, that you would have not been so upset with me, is that correct?"

In this strategic response, you're asking lots of questions about the criticism. This results in several consequences. First of all, it communicates to the person who is criticizing you that you're really listening. You're paying attention to what she is saying, and you are taking her very seriously. That alone may calm her down a little bit, since it makes it more likely that she will feel as though she is being attended to and that you are not being dismissive.

Secondly, and more importantly, even though you are still being criticized by somebody else, you are now directing the action. You are now determining what is being talked about and where that communication is going. Finally, this response makes it more likely that you will have a better understanding as to what it is that you're being criticized about so that it won't be a problem again in the future. But the thing most relevant here is the issue of control, so let's go back to that.

If someone is criticizing you, it will often feel like an out of control experience. When you direct the action yourself by asking for more information from the person who is doing the criticizing, such as "What is it about this that you're upset about?" "How could I have changed this?" or "What would you rather have had me do?" that will generally serve to help you feel a little bit more in control of the process and a little less anxious.

The OCD Connection

Cognitive exposure is a lot like that. Your client still experiences in his head the same thoughts or images that the OCD has been putting in there, but now *he's* putting those thoughts and images in there. *He's* creating it. *He's* the script writer, the architect, the engineer of the conversation in his head. And that sets up a different relationship between him and the symptom.

As an illustrative OCD case, let's say that Howard consistently uses his left hand to button his shirt in the morning when he gets dressed, because he fears that if he uses his right hand to button his shirt somehow this will result in his mother dying in a car accident . This kind of OCD obsession, where the feared consequence has no logical connection whatsoever to the obsession and just seems to be more of a superstition, is called OCD with "magical thinking." It is surprisingly common, and is found more often in children, who in general have more magical thinking whether or not they have OCD.

The exposure intervention in such a situation is for the clinician to contract with Howard to button his shirt with only his right hand, in opposition to what the OCD is telling him to do. Not only that, but while he is doing it, Howard is also to *imagine on purpose* that his mother is being killed in a car accident as a direct result of what he is doing. This is understandably very difficult and frightening for Howard to do, and so typically the therapist might have Howard do this in a hierarchal fashion, one small step at a time. He might have him start by writing a brief low intensity statement such as, "My mother might bump her arm today," or a general, more vague statement such as "Something not so good might happen to my Mom today," and would have him repeat this statement over and over again while he continued to button his shirt with his right hand and even after the behavior was completed. He would then, over time, progress to more detailed and more horrific scenarios, each time sticking with that scenario until he could button his shirt and say or read the statements with only very little anxiety.

You might tell the client, "Rather than waiting for the OCD to do it to you, *you* do it to you. And in so doing, you come to realize that the obsession doesn't really mean anything. It's just an OCD symptom."

"Rather than waiting for the OCD to do it to you, you do it to you."

This therapeutic strategy, sometimes called, "paradoxical intervention," or "prescribing the symptom," is something that may be applied to various psychological disorders. When a client complains to a cognitive behavioral therapist, "I'm having trouble sleeping, and even when I'm getting ready to go to sleep at night I start to get really anxious, because I think about how I'm going to be up all night again tossing and turning," paradoxical intervention is often the treatment suggested. Once medical/physiological causes have been ruled out, and other personal problems that might be contributing to this condition have been explored, cognitive behavioral therapists tend to prescribe a certain set of behavioral interventions to the client, such as instructions to abstain from daytime naps, follow a prescribed bedtime routine, and restrict the timing of eating, smoking, and drinking alcohol later in the day. Should these and additional behavioral interventions fail to provide relief from insomnia, the therapist might then resort to prescribing the symptoms by instructing the client to do the following:

"I'm going to make you a deal. I will tell you what you can do that will most probably help you to get rid of this problem. The deal is this: Tonight you do all the things you usually do when you go to bed. Prepare for bed, do the things you normally do for your bedtime routine, get into the bed, turn the light off, get under the covers, put your head on the pillow, close your eyes, and then do your best to *stay up all night*. Do not allow yourself to fall asleep."

With this assignment, you have turned everything upside-down. The anxiety about not falling asleep dissipates. Now the person is thinking, "How in the world am I going to stay up all night?" There is no longer pressure to fall asleep. And there is no way to fail. If the person stays up all night, he has followed the agreement. If he fails and falls asleep, well that is what he really wanted to do to begin with.

Paradoxical intervention can likewise be used with problems of male sexual dysfunction. Again, once medical, interpersonal, or other causes are ruled out, an assignment might be given to engage in sexual activity while trying to prevent oneself from attaining an erection. This serves in part to take the pressure off of performance. By doing that, it allows for performance anxiety to be reduced and for arousal to occur naturally.

Because sleep and sexual arousal are not things that you *make* happen, but rather they are things that happen *to you*, you cannot control those things directly. Like being criticized, you are essentially the recipient of an experience. When receiving criticism, by utilizing the skill of Asking For More, a person is able to obtain some aspect of control over his experience. The same thing can be said for the application of exposure therapy to the experience of OCD. You are teaching the client to switch from being the passive recipient of the obsessions to the creator of them. In so doing you help the client to gain mastery over the symptom.

You are teaching the client to switch from being the passive recipient of the obsessions to the creator of them.

Breathing

When introducing clients to relaxation training, it is often helpful to share information about why breathing is so often chosen as a component of these exercises. "When you think about it," the therapist might say, "a person's stress response, or anxiety response, is made up of a whole menu of physiological reactions, all designed to help that person behaviorally respond to the source of stress, either by physically fighting or defending against an attacker or by running away as fast as possible."

"This makes perfect sense, because until recently (in evolutionary terms, that is) things that stressed us out as human beings were not traffic jams and paying bills, but rather whether the guy down the road was going to club us to death or whether that saber toothed tiger was going to have us for lunch. Stress was a result of a pure physical threat, and so the 'fight or flight' reaction, as it has become known, was designed to help us better survive such a threat."

"Our breathing quickens in an effort to take in more oxygen, our heart rate increases in an effort to distribute that oxygen more quickly throughout the body. Blood vessels in our extremities constrict, and those in our brain and large muscle groups dilate, so that the blood that is rushing through our bodies is diverted to where it is needed most: our brains to think and our larger limbs to move. We don't need small finger dexterity when a large animal is chasing us down, and so, when reacting to stress, our faces get flushed, but our hands get icy cold. Likewise, in its infinite wisdom, the brain also shuts down most of the functions around digestion, diverting the blood away as if to say, 'While digestion is important for long term survival, it is not essential in the short term to help get through this emergency.' And so our mouths get try, our stomachs get upset, and we experience abdominal distress when under significant stress."

"A whole host of other automatic responses occur; our eyes dilate to let in more light, our hearing becomes more acute, and other neuromuscular and hormonal changes take place instantly, all without a conscious thought from us. In fact, almost all of these responses are not body functions that we can control directly at will. We can't usually exercise conscious control over our digestion process, blood flow, or heart rate (though it has been demonstrated that with such training as biofeedback, this is possible)."

"One of the exceptions to this statement, however, is breathing. Breathing is a body function that we don't have to think about. Like digestion and heart rate, it just occurs automatically without our conscious direction. Alternatively, however, we can choose to exercise direct control over it, holding it, speeding it up, slowing it down. And so it is also a voluntary action, like talking or walking. In this way, breathing becomes a 'conduit' between the world of involuntary functioning, where the fight or flight stress reaction resides, and the world of conscious control. It therefore becomes a natural choice as a point of impact on our anxiety responses."

And so this is how a therapist might introduce such exercises as paced breathing or diaphragmatic breathing to persons struggling with panic attacks, generalized anxiety disorder, or just plain, everyday stress. As a matter of course, many CBT therapists do *no*t focus on breathing retraining for OCD sufferers because this would be a form of neutralization of the anxiety, as opposed to exposure to anxiety. To be clear, it is not the point of this monologue on breathing exercises to encourage people to use breathing retraining, or any relaxation exercise for that matter, as an effective way of dealing directly with OCD anxiety.

Still, the concept of breathing control has a corollary in the understanding of obsessions and OCD.

The concept of breathing control has a corollary in the understanding of obsessions and OCD.

The OCD Connection

When a person experiences an obsession, it is as if a stream of thoughts bursts into one's consciousness without warning, without provocation from anything within, and most definitely without purposeful intent. Obsessions "happen" to people with OCD. They do not will an obsession. They are victimized by it. They do, however, as a natural response, tend to engage in compulsions in an attempt to lower the anxiety generated by the obsession.

When one engages in ERP, however, all that changes. The person now becomes an active participant in the production of the details of the obsession. He becomes the architect of the obsession, elaborating it, worsening it on purpose. And in so doing, he changes his relationship with the obsession from a passive recipient of the obsessive thought, to an active creator of it. The goal, of course, is to ultimately become its master, rather than its victim.

And so, the experience of an obsession has a parallel relationship to the experience of breathing. You can passively experience it and react to it, or you can construct, direct, and ultimately control it, by taking an aggressive stance. This strategy is espoused both in relaxation training for panic, anxiety, and stress, as well as in the proactive construction and exacerbation of obsessions in the treatment of OCD. As you encourage your clients to engage in ERP, it is important to continuously reinforce the idea of the power behind choosing to think beyond the obsession and instead encourage worsening the scenario in his head beyond what the OCD puts there. Discussing breathing retraining further illustrates how one can change one's relationship with obsessions from being a passive player to an active director of the action.

Predator and Prey

Near Albuquerque, New Mexico, there is a wonderful range of mountains you can drive up or climb called the Sandia Mountains. At the top of the main mountain, there is a little restaurant/gift shop. There, among the tee-shirts and knick-knacks, you will find a sign describing in detail what to do should one encounter a mountain lion in the area. For those of you who might visit from major metropolitan areas and have not recently spent much time in the wilderness, you might want to read that sign carefully. You would be surprised to find that running away or freezing and calling the "mountain lion police" on your cell phone (what would have been the first inclination for many a city-dweller) are not the recommended courses of action. Instead, the sign instructs the reader to stand his or her ground, look the beast right in the face, and make lots of noise, including growling, yelling, and hitting a tree with a stick. The instructions add that it might be helpful to wave your hands in the air, or even to take your jacket, if you had one, and hold it up high over your head, swinging it back and forth, in order to "look" bigger to the animal.

The OCD Connection

This brings to mind the behavioral treatment of OCD. The sign in the gift shop teaches the reader the basic lesson that if you *act* like prey (by freezing or running), the animal will *treat* you like prey and attack, feeling emboldened by your reaction to its threat. If on the other hand you respond like another predator, taking an attack/threatening stance, you stand a pretty good chance that the mountain lion will lose interest and turn away.

Likewise, if we think of OCD as the attacking mountain lion, we can respond as prey or as predator. If we behave like prey and "run" by avoiding OCD triggers, making attempts to reassure ourselves, or by acquiescing to the OCD behavioral demands, this serves only to invite the OCD to come after us with greater zeal and confidence, seeing us as the weak prey that we depict through our behavior. On the other hand, if we stand up to the OCD, and through behavioral exposure seek out the very triggers that stimulate our anxiety, and/or worsen our obsessions on purpose to undermine OCD's power over us, we are in "attack" mode. We will be viewed more as an adversarial predator rather than as prey. Then, like the big mountain lion in New Mexico, the OCD is more likely to turn and run.

Such a story serves to help motivate and embolden a hesitant or resistant client. It builds on the concept of changing one's attitude toward the OCD alluded to in some of the earlier stories, and developing a different relationship with it, one in which the client is no longer passively victimized by the disorder but is, instead, an active combatant bent on standing up to and challenging the OCD.

The client is no longer passively victimized by the disorder but is, instead, an active combatant bent on standing up to and challenging the OCD.

The Best Man

Jack is the best man at a wedding. He is renting a tuxedo from a store owned by his good friend Sol. As luck would have it, the tuxedo store is right down the block from the church where the wedding is to take place. This is fortunate because Jack has to work the day of the wedding and will need to rush to the church at the very last minute.

Jack arranges with Sol to drive his car to Sol's tuxedo store on the day of the wedding, just a few moments before the ceremony begins. Once there, he will give Sol his car keys, change from his work clothes into his tuxedo, leave his work clothes at the tuxedo store, and then just walk straight over to the church. Later on, after Sol closes up shop, he will drive the car to his own home, and Jack will find a ride home with someone from the wedding party.

The day of the wedding arrives. Jack drives to Sol's store, gives him the keys to the car, and changes his clothes in the fitting room of the tuxedo store as planned. While Jack is changing clothes, Sol gets a phone call and finds that he needs to leave immediately. He calls out to Jack, "Jack, I have an emergency and I have to run! I'm locking up, so when you leave and the door closes behind you, the alarm will automatically set, and the doors will lock. You won't be able to get back in, so make sure you have everything you need when you exit the store. I am taking your car." Jack calls out "OK," and thanks Sol for helping him out. Sol leaves. Jack emerges from the fitting room and leaves his clothes in the tuxedo store as planned, exits from the store, and closes the door behind him. He is about to walk down the street to the church. But Jack now finds that he is faced with a dilemma.

Two things have created a set of circumstances that now challenge our friend Jack. First, during the time that Jack spent changing into his tux, there was a brief rain storm. It's not raining now, but there are dirty puddles all over the place. Second, Jack's friend who is getting married is a little eccentric, and all the outfits in the wedding party are completely white. Jack's tuxedo, including his tie, is all white. His shirt is white, his socks, his shoes, and even the soles of the shoes are white.

Jack has got to get to that church quickly, because they are going to start taking pictures of the wedding party any time now, but of course he is concerned about getting dirty. He starts to head toward the church, walking very carefully, very deliberately. He looks down in front of him, scanning ahead for any muddy puddles that might soil his outfit. He takes a few steps, and then notices that he has a small droplet of muddy water clinging to the side of the sole of one of his shoes. He takes his thumb, tries to gently rub off the droplet, but instead creates a long smudge on the side of his shoe. He feels himself getting very anxious, and he thinks to himself, "This is terrible! What am I going to do?" He walks even more slowly, more carefully, in an attempt to avoid any further dirtying of his tuxedo.

Jack continues to take a few more steps, and as he lifts one foot, another muddy droplet falls from the foot lifted onto the top of his other shoe. Again Jack attempts to wipe it clean with his finger, and again the result is yet another smudge, this time right there on the top of his shoe. Jack's anxiety skyrockets, and he worries that he will not look presentable for photographs by the time he reaches the church.

But Jack is determined. He walks even more slowly, and works his hardest to carefully survey the sidewalk in front of him as he makes his way down the street. He feels anxious, and all the time he is worrying to himself, "If I am not careful, I will get even more dirty and look terrible! I will ruin the wedding photographs! The bride and groom will be angry with me! I must be very, very careful!" As he walks, he notices that the bottom part of one of his pant legs has become soiled. His heart sinks, but he remains steadfast in his quest to traverse the minefield of puddles between himself and the church and get there on time, looking presentable for the photographer.

After what seems like many long, excruciating, almost painful steps toward the church, Jack looks up and sees it nearly right in front of him. It is on the corner of the next block, and all he has to do is cross the street. He looks down at his legs and shoes, and sees that they really don't look so bad after all. Chances are no one will even notice the tiny smudges. He breathes a sigh of relief and braces himself for the last few careful strides toward the church.

But at the very second that Jack places his first foot off the curb and into the street, in that brief moment when he shifts his weight onto that foot and begins to move himself forward across the few yards that separate him from the steps leading to the church door, in that split second, a car races around the corner, seemingly coming out of nowhere, barrels down the very street that Jack has just begun to cross, zooms right in front of him, nearly hitting him, and then just as quickly disappears around the next corner.

A moment later, once Jack has caught his breath and his balance and is about to redirect his attention back to the last few yards of his journey, he realizes what has just happened. When that car ran right in front of him, it also ran into a puddle, and sprayed him from head to toe with muddy water. Jack is horrified and shocked. Now what?

No time to change. No other tux to change into anyway, as the tuxedo store is locked and the alarm is on. There are only two options. Find another way to get home and not show for the wedding altogether, or suck it up and show up as he is, mud-covered and all. The former does not really seem like an option for Jack, so it's off to church in his muddied outfit.

But things are different now. First, he is no longer walking slowly and carefully. He can sprint to the church stairs and up to the door. There is no further need to worry and be careful about getting dirty. It is already a done deal. There is no turning back. And by accepting the situation as it exists, by accepting that he is going to this wedding in a muddied tuxedo and there is nothing he can do about it, Jack is able to let go of the pressure to try to keep the suit pristine. There is no longer any anxiety about getting dirty, because he already *is* dirty.

There is no longer any anxiety about getting dirty, because he already is *dirty.*

Although he is upset that he is now completely dirty, and he may be worried about the reaction of the rest of the wedding party and guests when they see his mud-sprayed tux at the wedding, he is no longer worried and anxious about the *possibility* of getting muddied. He already *is* muddied. And so in some strange way, this course of events has "freed" Jack of his anxiety, his obsessive review in his mind of the need to walk carefully, and his slow, avoidant walking ritual.

The OCD Connection

What has happened in this story to Jack is very much like the transformation that you will witness taking place in your clients who challenge themselves with ERP exercises. In the beginning stages of ERP, when your clients have just begun to challenge their OCD by doing "forbidden" acts of some kind, there is the temptation to fantasize that somehow they may be able to reverse what they have done, "fix" it in some way, and once again appease the OCD. But holding on to the idea that one can "undo" an ERP experience becomes more and more difficult over the course of the exposure, because the OCD client realizes that it would be more unlikely that he will actually be able to completely reverse the situation created by the exposure. There is a sense that one will get "overwhelmed" by all that is required to turn back the clock and make things the way they were. What ultimately happens at this point, however, is that there is a letting go of the fantasy that things *can* be "put back the way they were" so that the OCD is appeased. This "letting go" of the fantasy of being able to make things go back to the way they were is the very mechanism that allows for the lowering of anxiety in the ERP process.

As an illustration, let us assume Phil believes that his car is contaminated. His home, however is not contaminated. In order to keep his home in its "clean" state, whenever he drives home from somewhere, Phil immediately strips off all his clothes when he walks through the front door and then takes a shower. Afterwards, he carefully brings the contaminated clothes to his laundry room and washes them, careful to wash his hands thoroughly afterwards since they had been recontaminated by his touching the clothes.

Exposure therapy might involve having Phil go to his car in an uncontaminated state. He would then touch a part of his car that might not feel quite as contaminated as, let's say, the drive's seat, which might feel like the "hottest" site of contamination in the car. So for example, we might have him touch the rear bumper. This might produce some anxiety, but not a terribly high amount. Phil would then engage in what is called "touch and spread" ERP. After touching the bumper, he would then "spread" the contamination that he feels on his hands all over his "pristine" house, contaminating it.

At first, Phil would feel relatively high anxiety as he touched the inside doorknob of his front door, and began to touch the furniture in his living room. He might imagine that he could, at a later time, go back and wipe down these items, cleaning the contamination off of them. As he continues to touch more and more items in his house, however, his anxiety may actually rise. He begins to think how difficult it will be to remember everything he touched and how hard it would be to clean everything.

Once he is instructed to touch the walls, the carpeting, various articles of clothing in his closet and chest of drawers, a few of his kitchen utensils, some items in his linen closet, and some papers in his file cabinet, Phil comes to the realization that he could never be sure that he had completely decontaminated the house, even if he spent days trying to clean everything. There were just too many things. He would never remember everything he had touched.

And so something interesting happens to Phil. He lets go of the fantasy that he can undo his ERP. This creates a sense of loss and defeat that may make him feel briefly sad, but it is accompanied by the complete release of the experience of anxiety. He no longer stresses about decontaminating the house. He accepts this as an impossibility, and so he lets go of worrying about how he will clean it all up. Just as Jack the best man was free to run the rest of the way to the church without worrying if he would get any more dirty from muddy puddles, Phil can now touch anything else that is in the house with his contaminated hands without experiencing increased anxiety. Both men have become free from obsessing about how to avoid or how they will undo. Their stress levels plummet.

With regard to those initial sad feelings of loss, we expect that those will dissipate rather rapidly for Phil, especially as he approaches the point where he can drive his car home and then enter his house without any anxiety or need to wash. The freedom, time, and energy saved, the increased sense of power and control, and the lack of emotional stress will have replaced any feelings of loss or defeat that he may have experienced initially. As for our friend Jack, we can only hope that he had a great time at the wedding and that the story of how he came to the occasion with a white tuxedo full of mud stains will serve as a story that he and his friends will laugh about for years to come.

Therapists can utilize The Best Man story to help motivate clients in the early stages of ERP work. It is another illustration of why the person with OCD should resist trusting the "voice" in his head that tells him that the task at hand will be too overwhelming and that he will fail. The story proposes that this voice is a misconception, and it explains the psychological dynamics of why this is so. Helping clients to envision themselves successfully negotiating an exposure protocol is key to assisting them in starting the process. Their resistance to engaging in behavioral exposure is often rooted in the fact that they don't think they will be able to "go all the way" with it and that they will get overwhelmed. The Best Man story is an excellent way to relay the message that ultimately getting overwhelmed leads to a "surrendering" of sorts by clients and that this "giving up" process paradoxically empowers them and frees them from OCD control.

Helping clients to envision themselves successfully negotiating an exposure protocol is key to assisting them in starting the process.

Chemistry Exam

Imagine that you are in your sophomore year of high school, and, like most of your friends, you are well practiced in the art of procrastination when it comes to studying for tests. On this particular occasion, you begin studying for a major chemistry exam at 8 o'clock the night before the exam is to be given. You have not yet started to do anything in preparation for this test, and you are understandably quite anxious about how things might turn out. As you begin studying, it becomes clearer that it is going to be a significant challenge to absorb all the information that is required in just the few hours remaining that evening.

The hours pass, and your anxiety grows. Armed with a kettle for boiling water and some instant coffee, you attempt to cram your burning brain with as much information as possible while staving off anxiety-laden thoughts of failure. The clock strikes midnight, and you begin to panic. Surely, you will never be ready in time. Should you call in sick? What would you tell your parents? What would be your excuse for the teacher? Could you feign illness?

You find yourself reading certain paragraphs over and over, as your concentration deteriorates and your mind fills with thoughts alternating between schemes to avoid the impending disaster and visions of the horrible consequences should you end up taking the test and failing. Despite your standard operating procedure of leaving things to the last minute, you have always ended up doing OK in school. But this time you have pushed the envelope too far. By 1 a.m. you find yourself not even looking at the textbook and just staring into space, your mind racing with self-talk. "Stupid! Stupid! Stupid!!! What was I thinking? I had done so well, and now I am going to blow it! There must be a way out of this! Maybe the test will be cancelled. Maybe there will be a snow day. Maybe the teacher will get sick, and they will decide to postpone the exam until she gets back!"

You begin to try to strike a deal with the Almighty, contracting that if you could get out of this mess, you will never, ever procrastinate in this manner again. You find yourself feeling physically ill, nauseated, and dizzy, and of course, very, very tired. You vacillate between feelings of anger at yourself on the one hand and frustration for not being able to come up with a solution to your problem on the other. But most of all, you experience anticipatory anxiety about taking that test. You dread waking up in the morning and feel weak at the knees just thinking about walking into that classroom. In between this roller coaster of emotion and thought, you find yourself making short, furious attempts at studying.

By 2:30 in the morning, it is over. You have concluded that you are, indeed, going to fail the test. It is time to go to sleep and deal with tomorrow when tomorrow comes. And then something curious happens.

You no longer feel anxious. It is as if a yoke of burden has been lifted from your shoulders. You are still thinking to yourself that you will in all likelihood fail, and you do feel sad about this, but the anticipatory anxiety is gone. In your mind, you have already failed the exam. It is a done deal. You can no longer entertain the possibility that you will escape the dreaded consequences, so there is no need to work so hard to try to avoid them. You have surrendered to the inevitable and in so doing, surprisingly, freed your mind. You are able to go to bed, fall asleep quickly, and sleep soundly through the night. You are no longer tortured by the prospect of possible failure, because it is no longer a question in you mind. You have, in fact, surrendered your quest to somehow "get away with it." The train had already left the station, and you were not on it. There is nothing you can do about it, but accept the reality of the situation.

You have surrendered to the inevitable and in so doing, surprisingly, freed your mind.

The OCD Connection

A similar process takes place during the exposure experience of ERP. Consider the client who has the obsession that the police are going to storm his house one day armed with a search and seizure warrant and claim that he had downloaded child pornography. In this particular case, the man had not actually downloaded any child pornography.

The client had in fact used a credit card to purchase entrance to a regular pornography site on one occasion, and this history was enough to fuel his obsessive anxiety. Had he given his credit card number to a child pornography site by accident? Had his card number somehow been rerouted to make it look as though he had purchased child pornography? Did he in fact, perhaps by accident, stumble across a child porn site without realizing it, even though he may not recall having done that specifically?

This man would call his credit card companies and then call them again, checking if there were any extraneous charges that might lead to his arrest and incarceration. He closed his credit card accounts and opened new, fresh accounts. He physically destroyed several of his computers. He would ruminate constantly; was he guilty? Will they come? What will his family think? What will be the reaction of his professional colleagues? Would there be a court case? Who would he choose as a lawyer? Where might he be incarcerated?

He would spend hour after hour, day after day, reviewing all these "What if?" questions, sometimes researching lawyers or legal issues around those who have been accused in the past. He was clearly tortured and terrified. What makes this particular obsessive-compulsive cycle so resilient is that, even if no police would come for weeks, months, or years, they still, in this client's mind, could come *some* day. In fact, as time passes, rather than being reassured that nothing will indeed happen, this client becomes *more* convinced that the time of his arrest and incarceration is drawing nearer.

Ultimately, the breakthrough comes when he concludes that the police will in fact come for him some day, that he will be found guilty and go to jail, that his life will be over from that point on, and there is nothing that he could do now or ever to change that. All that is left is for him to live his life as best as he can with the time that remains. It is not unlike any other person accepting the inevitability of death. The event is definitely coming, though you don't know when. You can't avoid it. The best you can do is accept it.

In no longer trying to "fix" the situation and avoid the dreaded outcome, paradoxically, the man's anxiety dramatically drops. This surrender to the "inevitable" frees his mind, allowing him to move forward in his life. It is one of those strange, counterintuitive aspects of OCD and its treatment, in that by surrendering over to the OCD obsession, you can in fact weaken, debilitate, or even destroy it. You can utilize Chemistry Exam as a common collective experience that nearly all clients will be able to personally relate to. By using the story to illustrate the dynamics of paradoxical surrender, you help encourage your client to move forward in his ERP challenges, by providing the perspective that he will reach a point where his anxiety will significantly drop via acceptance of the conditions created by exposure.

Eating Brussels Sprouts

A child psychologist taught classes at the local college. When undergraduates came to visit him on campus they were greeted by all kinds of child-friendly things all around his office: games, toys, and a variety of kids' posters hanging all over the walls.

One poster in particular held a prominent position at the center of the back wall behind the professor's desk. At the bottom of the poster was a drawing of a bowl of Brussels sprouts, seemingly done by a small child with different colored crayons. At the top of the poster, above the bowl of Brussels sprouts, again written in crayon and appearing in a child's handwriting, was written the following; "I'm glad I hate Brussels sprouts, because if I liked'em, I'd eat lots of'em, and I hate'em!"

Let us examine where the error in thinking lies. The child imagines that she is existing at some time in the future. In that future she imagines that, because she has come to like Brussels sprouts, she is now eating lots of them. The problem is, once she says it, she focuses on the fact that she is eating lots of Brussels sprouts, but *not* on the fact that she is doing so because she likes them. She sees herself, in the future, as *she is now*, that is, hating Brussels sprouts, but eating lots of them, and, being a child, that grosses her out.

The OCD Connection

Twisted thinking is at the heart of what sometimes gets in the way of progress in cases of OCD.

Twisted thinking is at the heart of what sometimes gets in the way of progress in cases of OCD. It is what often keeps OCD clients from moving forward in their ERP therapies. Let's consider

Nadine, a young woman with OCD who has her own version of this child's statement. "The OCD keeps me afraid of 'letting go' of the fear," she says, "because if I let go, I might do the things that I am afraid of doing."

The piece of the puzzle that is missing in her logic, of course, is the fact that if she let go of the fear of doing the things that she was *presently* afraid of doing, it would be because she was *no longer afraid* of doing them! She has projected herself into the future in terms of the behavior, that is, doing things she is now afraid of, but has not projected into the future a sense of herself after having let go of the fear. She sees herself as she is *now*, unchanged, doing the things she would be doing in the future, while she misses the important idea that she would *only* be doing those things in the future because she had, in fact, undergone a change in herself. She will have let go of the fear, increasing her level of trust or risk tolerance, or both.

Ultimately, the response to this struggle is to help the client focus on her present challenges. Encourage your clients not to think of the process of recovery as taking place too much in the future. Instruct them to take things one step at a time, or as those in the addictions recovery say, "One day at a time." Demonstrate to your clients that it would be silly for a child learning his multiplication table in grade school to worry about how he will handle college calculus. But very often this is exactly what OCD clients do.

A particularly effective opportunity to utilize the Brussels Sprouts story in therapy occurs when you are presented with a client such as a middle-aged woman whom we shall call Rhonda. Rhonda has successfully challenged her contamination fears at several levels, yet each time she is challenged with the next level, she is overwhelmed by anxiety that she will "change her mind" later on, and will not be able to "undo" the contamination that she has spread all over the place.

What is interesting in the case of Rhonda is that she is never concerned about being able to spread the contamination *now*, in fact she states that she is quite confident that she could do so without much emotional discomfort. In fact, when she engaged in exposure trials in the past she experienced relatively low levels of anxiety. Still, she hesitates taking the next step. What stalls her is the idea that *later on*, she will suddenly be sorry that she spread the contamination, get overwhelmed with anxiety, and then be unable to "fix" everything by getting it all back to a precontaminated state. Invariably, of course, this doesn't happen, but it is hard to convince clients of that when they are feeling the fear. The story of Brussels Sprouts helps to remind them that they cannot accurately project themselves into the future and guess at what they will be capable of handling. When they are further down the line behaviorally, in terms of being able to engage in behaviors that are presently prohibited by OCD, they will also have experienced changes within themselves, becoming stronger and more resistant to OCD-generated fears.

Color Blind

James is a kid in your high school who is color blind. You never gave much thought to how this might have affected his life (though there were a few times when his clothes were poorly matched), until one day you find yourself a passenger in his car. While he is driving, it suddenly hits you—how does he know whether the traffic light is green or red? (Although there are different variations of color blindness, you know from conversations with James that these were the two colors he often confused.) He explains in a matter-of-fact way that he *couldn't* tell what color the lights were, and he only knew when to stop or go while driving depending on what part of the traffic light was lit up. When the top light was lit, he knew it was red, when the bottom one was lit, he knew it was green.

James doesn't react to what he sees (at least in terms of colors) but to what he knows to be the truth. James can't control whether he sees green or red, but he can control his thoughts about the lights he sees in the traffic signal. Even though to his eyes, the bottom light looks identical to the top one, he trusts that it really is green, and controls his behavior by continuing to drive through the intersection. Not only that, his complete trust in the fact that the light really *is* green even though he cannot tell this by the color itself, allows him to drive through the intersection confidently and with no anxiety associated with it. It is this faith, this belief in the fact that if the bottom light of the traffic signal is lit up, then it is green, even though he cannot see this with his own eyes, that enables him to drive through without the anxiety.

The OCD Connection

The OCD client cannot directly control the obsession that enters her mind—"I might have hit somebody with my car on the road back there," she thinks. "What if I poisoned that person because I didn't adequately wash my hands before touching him?" she wonders. But she *can* learn to trust that the thoughts are symptoms of the OCD and not representations of reality, as real as they may seem.

James had the benefit of seeing where in the traffic signal the light was lit, and that cued him in to whether the color was green or red. However, for the rest of us, our response to traffic lights are not dependent on what part of the light is lit up, only on the color that we see. Because James did not have the ability to distinguish these colors, he had to trust that colors were what he knew them to be, not what he saw. Likewise, the person with OCD has to trust that her thoughts are what she knows them to be, that is, OC symptoms, and not what they appear to be, that is, true representations of dangers in her world.

She can *learn to trust that the thoughts are symptoms of the OCD and not representations of reality.*

As a therapist assisting your client in exposure work, your first step is usually to help the client label the thought as an OCD thought. This is like James labeling what he sees (or more accurately, what he *doesn't* see) as a byproduct of his color blindness and not as a representation of what is out there in the real world. It is no doubt a very difficult thing to not trust your own eyes, but this is the challenge at hand. Another illustration of this appears in a popular film from the late 1990s.

In *The Matrix*, Neo, the main character, learns that he is living in a completely fabricated universe, wherein nothing that he sees or physically experiences through his senses actually exists, but rather his life has all along been a running computer program that is being fed into his brain. In the movie, once this fact is recognized, once a person knows that nothing is real but just a virtual computer program, one has the ability to change the laws governing this fabricated universe and attain all kinds of superhuman abilities, such as defying the law of gravity—just jump off a building, and you keep moving forward. The trick is, you have to really *believe* that what you are seeing is actually not real. If you slip and even for a moment forget that fact, you fall prey to the laws of the universe—jump off a building, and you fall down.

In the film, Neo meets a youngster who has mastered this challenge. The boy looks at a spoon, and, at his will, it bends and floats in the air. "How do you do that?" asks Neo. "You have to remember," says the boy, "there *is* no spoon." Later in the film, when Neo is faced with a death-defying jump, you can hear him mumble to himself, "There is no spoon," in an effort to remind himself that, however real the danger appears, this is all the fabrication of that computer program being downloaded in his head, nothing is really happening as it appears to be, and there is no real danger.

This is the challenge facing your OCD clients. Recognizing and trusting that the danger, no matter how real its may appear, is actually the fabrication of the OCD, is an essential step in disregarding the danger. Once done, then, like jumping off the building and safely flying, the OCD client can better drive on without going back to check for accident victims, or not wash to prevent contamination, or not touch something a certain number of times, all with confidence that all will be fine and that there is no danger, because "there is no spoon."

Peanuts

We are all familiar with it. It usually is displayed prominently on the first page of the Sunday funnies. Charles Shultz's Charlie Brown comic strip, lovingly titled "Peanuts." If you have followed the comic over the years, or have seen some of the TV holiday specials, you may recall some of the main recurring themes in the Peanuts world. There is the little curly red-headed girl that Charlie Brown worships from afar, the unrequited love that Lucy experiences towards the pianist, Schroeder, and Linus's annual Halloween evening in the pumpkin patch, where he waits, year after year, for the arrival of the "Great Pumpkin," never failing to get disappointed. There is Snoopy's fantasy of being the Red Baron, Charlie Brown standing on the pitcher's mound in the pouring rain outraged that the other kids have left the field, Lucy's psychiatrist office, and Linus's affection for his ever present blanket. And so much more.

But for now let us focus on one of the smaller dynamics of the Peanuts world—Lucy, Charlie Brown, and the football. The scenario typically runs this way: Lucy asks if she can hold the football edge up on the ground so that Charlie Brown can take a running start and kick the ball out from under her hand, sending it flying across the football field. Charlie Brown refuses, claiming that each time Lucy offers to do this favor for him, she whisks the ball away at the last second, just as Charlie Brown is about to strike it with his foot, causing him to fly skyward, and end up flat on his back.

With the sincerity of an angel and the persuasiveness of a lawyer, Lucy somehow convinces Charlie Brown, that, finally this time, she will indeed hold the football in place, allowing him to make contact with it. He caves in and agrees. She holds it, he runs for it, and, as she has done a million times before, she removes the ball at the very last second and Charlie Brown ends up lying face up on the ground. The last box in the strip usually has Lucy making some flippant remark, such as "You are just too gullible, Charlie Brown."

We read these comic installments time after time, hoping against hope that Charlie Brown will use his common sense and not believe Lucy's promises, but to no avail. He always does, and she always follows through by removing that football in the last second before contact. We might ask ourselves, "Why does he keep falling for the same trick?" "Why does he believe her if she consistently dupes him?" "Hasn't he heard of that old expression, 'Fool me once—shame on you; fool me twice—shame on me?'"

The OCD Connection

The truth is, sometimes it's hard to question a persuasive argument; just ask anyone with OCD. People with OCD are a lot like Charlie Brown. They believe someone who cannot be trusted. They believe someone who always lies to them. They believe their OCD. At a certain level, OCD talks to the person afflicted with it. It gives orders, threatens, persuades, and intimidates. It doesn't just throw out the question, "What if?" If you dig a little below the surface, the OCD is also essentially saying, "And if you don't try to get to the answer of the 'What if?' question, if you don't try to make things 'just right,' if you don't try to become sure, to make the feelings of discomfort go away, then something terrible will happen, or I'll make your life so miserable that you won't be able function forever, and you won't be able to handle it!"

Sometimes it's hard to question a persuasive argument; just ask anyone with OCD.

And the person with OCD gives in. He gives in because he believes the OCD threats. More than any other, that last threat, the threat that he will become overwhelmed with emotional discomfort for an infinite amount of time and won't be able to "take it," is the one that gets him to cave in. People with OCD find it incredibly difficult to not trust this feeling, even when they have successfully challenged the OCD many times before, and it was clearly demonstrated that they did in fact get over that initial spike of anxiety, that they did for the most part recover, that they were able to move on with their lives, even though they fought back and did not engage in the compulsive reaction. I say "for the most part" because sometimes the lingering doubt or concern can last for a very long time, but I am very quick to point out that in those long-term lingering stages of doubt, the person's functioning is usually not really impacted.

People with OCD often have in their own personal experience and memory proof that the OCD lies. They know that they have not engaged in the ritualistic response to an obsession and have been able to withstand the resulting discomfort, and that, with the passage of time, have been able to let go of that particular obsession, at least to the point that they could function (although sometimes this is hard to see because their functioning has become threatened by a new obsession-driven fear). And yet, for whatever reason, when a new challenge arises, they doubt themselves and their ability to tolerate the discomfort. They believe those OCD lies about what will happen if they don't engage in the tempting ritual.

It is like Charlie Brown experiencing over and over again Lucy's promise, the breaking of that promise, and the resulting humiliation. Yet once again, he chooses to respond to her promise as if the past did not exist. He does not learn from his experience. He concludes that *this* time it *will* be different. Of course, in reality there is nothing to differentiate *this* particular instance from all the others in the past, and Lucy pulls the football away at the very last moment.

And so it is with OCD. It is believed when it shouldn't be trusted. It is submitted to when it should be challenged—when it *can* be challenged. Fortunately, life is not like a comic strip. As we have been discussing through many narratives in this book, people can successfully face their fears. It is a matter of knowing where to place your trust. As a clinician, it is your obligation to help your OCD client place that trust in himself, in his own memory of successful challenges to his OCD, in his ability to withstand, persevere, and ultimately overcome whatever emotional curveballs the OCD throws at him. Remembering that this discomfort is often short-lived and is always ultimately quite manageable are important ideas to emphasize in assisting the client in his battle plan against obsessive compulsive urges. It is important for him to remember that after successfully challenging the OCD and not giving in to the compulsive behavior, he can look back afterward and feel empowered, strengthened, and renewed in hope and anticipation for triumphs yet to come.

It's that wonderful feeling of confidence and self-fulfillment that one gets after doing well on that most difficult school exam, or getting that applause at the close of the piano recital, or watching that football take off after striking it at just the right angle with your foot and finding your heart racing with exhilaration as you find yourself scoring the field goal.

Temper Tantrum

You are in the mall and hear some screaming while inside one of the stores. You walk to the front of the store, and see the following scene: A woman, about 30 years old, is standing in the middle of the mall walkway, leaning on the railing that surrounds the opening in the middle of the floor where you can look down to the mall level below you. In front of her is a large stroller, on the back of which hangs several shopping bags. On the floor in front of her, right there in the middle of the mall hallway, is a child, about three years old. She is sitting with her legs spread out in a V configuration, screaming at the top of her lungs. Tears are rolling down her cheeks, cheeks which have become quite flushed with her incessant crying. She is shouting something unintelligible, and every few seconds the intensity of her screams increases, and she pounds her fists on the hard floor, as if to further drive home the point she is trying to make.

The woman, who you assume is the child's mother because you are able to make out the word "Mommy" a couple of times somewhere within the child's screams, stands calmly by watching this scene and doing nothing. At first you are taken aback—why isn't she doing anything? Why isn't she trying to calm this child who was obviously in distress? Are you witnessing, right here in the middle of the mall walkway, an example of extreme child neglect?

Within a few seconds you realize that the mother is merely dealing with a toddler's temper tantrum in a manner that many a parent would see as responsible and effective. She is ignoring it. She is patiently waiting for the child to calm down, for as long as it takes, before she intervenes and tries to make things better. At that point, once the child had calmed down, she might attempt to reason with the child or in some way have an interaction with her.

This is similar to the "time out" technique that so many parents have employed after they find that any attempt to have an interaction with a screaming child, short of giving her exactly what she wants, results in even more screaming. The philosophy is that you are essentially teaching the child that screaming and yelling do not result in getting attention, consolation, or whatever it is that she wants. She needs to find other, more appropriate ways to ask for what she needs, or to let the parent know when she is unhappy or angry about something. This approach of course is not uniformly agreed on by either parents or child experts. But it is subscribed to by many a parent, and most of them feel comfortable with the choice of this approach.

This philosophy is often difficult to execute, especially for less experienced parents. There is the concern that they are torturing the child. They worry that they are withholding love, comfort, and validation, and that this may somehow result in some long-lasting psychological damage that will take years of therapy to rectify. Then of course there is the embarrassment of the acting-out behavior taking place in a public arena and the fear that people will judge them as being ineffective parents, thinking that they are being neglectful, just as you might have done when you first witnessed the scene.

But this mother is calm and resolute in her decision to stand and wait. She does not seem at all concerned that other shoppers might think badly of her or that she is dealing inappropriately with the situation. She does not react to the screams, because she understands, it seems, that she does not have to, and that in fact reacting to the screams might reinforce them in some way, resulting in screaming becoming a more regular reaction on the part of the child whenever she felt frustrated or denied.

Reacting to the screams might reinforce them in some way, resulting in screaming becoming a more regular reaction on the part of the child.

Ultimately, the crying stops, and the child calms down. At that point, the mother approaches her, bends down and speaks softly to her, places her into the stroller, and they go on their way together.

The OCD Connection

And so it is with OCD. When a client has an obsession, when the thought enters her mind that she must engage in a certain ritual, whatever it may be, any attempt to ignore the thought, to withhold from engaging in the ritual, any action or inaction on her part that is designed to deny the wishes of the OCD monster in her head will result in what is essentially a temper tantrum. The OCD will scream at the top of its lungs, threatening, demanding that she submit to its will. With a direct or implied threat, it vows to torture her until she gives in to it, it threatens to keep her from being able to do anything else until she behaves exactly as it has directed. It tries to hold her prisoner until she does as she has been told.

The image that your client might find helpful is one of the toddler in the midst of a temper tantrum. Like OCD, she makes a lot of noise, she is annoying, and she can at times be embarrassing. She often keeps your client from her shopping or from engaging in other activities, and she seems to threaten that she will keep it up until your client gives in to her demands.

The therapist can use the Temper Tantrum story to illustrate how the OCD isn't really in control, but the client is, just as was the case with the mother in our story. Secure, confident, and informed parents remember that *they* are still the parents. They do not have to react to the temper tantrum. They can remain calm and optimistic that this will pass and that the child will get the message that temper tantrums will not get her what she wants. By ignoring her screams and patiently waiting for her to stop, parents can exercise their inherent power over the child. The screams will stop, eventually, and be less likely to occur the next time.

The same holds true for exercising one's control over the OCD. Just like the child, your client cannot order her OCD to stop screaming at her—she does not have that kind of direct control. But she can get it to weaken, and ultimately even stop, if she chooses not to respond, and patiently wait for it to get tired of screaming. Help the client to anthropomorphize the OCD, and to trust that it is only having a temper tantrum and that is all. Support her in remaining resolute in not caving in and giving in to its demands. Encourage her to remain calm and optimistic that, just like the mom at the mall, she will ultimately be rewarded for her patience and determination.

Paper Tiger

You live alone in an apartment. You have had a few fish, a couple of turtles, and a parakeet as pets in the past but have never shared your home with a nonhuman mammal—no cats, no dogs, not even a guinea pig.

A co-worker whom you have befriended asks you to cat-sit for her while she is on vacation for two weeks, and you agree. The feline, named Sunny, is quite beautiful, has long golden fur, and, according to her owner, possesses a very sweet disposition.

So the big day arrives, and you await your new temporary roommate. Your friend brings Sunny in, and she immediately runs under your living-room sofa. There she stays for the duration of your friend's hour-long visit, and does not come out, even at the urging of her owner. Your friend has to grab her gently from under the couch so she could show her where you would be placing the litter box and her food, but immediately upon putting her back down on the floor, Sunny is off again and flies under the couch. Your friend leaves, reassuring you that you just need to be patient and that Sunny would ultimately adapt to her new surroundings. And off she goes.

Sunny stays under the couch for hours. She slowly begins to venture forth and spends the rest of the afternoon and evening exploring every crack and crevice of your apartment. Eventually she seems to make herself comfortable, and uses her litter box, food, and water bowls as needed. You find however, that whenever you enter a room that she is in, she either leaves immediately or runs out of sight somewhere. Every attempt on your part to engage her fails.

Finally, after about four days, you make it your goal to make physical contact with her. You try to cajole her from under the sofa chair, and when that doesn't work, you reach under to grab her, as her owner had done, only to have her shoot out from underneath the chair. You chase after her from one part of the apartment to the other, and at one point you trap her in a corner of the room with no place to hide. You place your body between her and any other escape route and begin to approach her slowly, talking gently to her as you do so.

As you get closer, all of sudden, this beautiful, gentle looking animal turns terribly ugly. She arches her back up high, her fur seems to stand up on edge, she bares her teeth, and hisses very loudly at you in the most threatening way. This automatic response to your approach, designed to deter any possible threat, does the job. You retreat, and decide to let Sunny call the shots from that point on. As it works out, she is sitting in your lap as you watch TV by the end of the week.

But thinking back on these events, you are surprised to find that, in the safety of your own home, you felt, for that one moment when the cat called on her instinctual defenses, truly afraid and threatened. She had really scared you, and your backing up response was less of a calculated move on your part but, rather, *your* automatic, instinctual response designed to protect yourself. What really caught you by surprise was how a seemingly placid, defenseless animal seemed so powerful and menacing (she was an indoor cat and had been declawed at a time when cat owners had this done more regularly than today).

Of course, Sunny's display had been just a show. She was, in fact, still pretty defenseless and powerless. You were much bigger than she, although slower, for sure, and you were never in any real danger. Yet your own reaction demonstrated that you had in fact been fooled by her display of aggressiveness. She was in fact what we refer to as a paper tiger—menacing in appearance and presentation but fragile and powerless in reality.

She was in fact what we refer to as a paper tiger*—menacing in appearance and presentation but fragile and powerless in reality.*

The OCD Connection

And there is the OCD connection. In the same way that years of evolution have created an animal that can make itself appear more threatening than it really is as a natural defense against predators or combatants, OCD has been engineered to create the illusion that it, too, is more powerful than it is in reality. Often, when someone with OCD makes an attempt to stand up to it, to challenge it, or to ignore it, the OCD symptom intensifies. It becomes more threatening, raising the stakes of noncompliance, as if to say, "You better do as I say, or else ..."

To continue our analogy, if, as therapists treating OCD through exposure work, we continue to anthropomorphize the OCD, as we have been throughout this book, it appears as though the OCD gets angry at the client who challenges it, and bares its teeth in an effort to get the person back in line. And this usually works. The client will back off, engage in the demanded ritual, and the status quo actually now worsens: the dominance of the OCD is solidified. Paper Tiger is a story that may help you to illustrate this dynamic to your clients as a way of helping them to reframe the spike in anxiety that they will often feel when moving forward in their exposure work.

This dynamic is very much like the interaction between Sunny and the cat sitter. The OCD roars louder, bares its teeth, and becomes more threatening, not so much because it is demonstrating its true position of dominance, but because, like Sunny, the OCD is feeling threatened. It knows that if the client stands up to it, challenges it, and is unwavering in his or her resoluteness to disobey the OCD's commands, that ultimately, the OCD will be revealed for what it really is: completely helpless to do anything. A fraud. A phony. A bully without a backbone.

It is as if the OCD understands that it must, at all costs, keep the client believing that he or she cannot stand up to it, that the OCD will ultimately prevail, and that there is no option but to give in. It can survive only as long as it can perpetuate the illusion that the client is helpless in the face of OCD. And so it is important to see OCD's reaction to a challenge, not so much as a demonstration of power and authority, but as a survival reaction of an animal that itself is feeling threatened. It is the OCD that feels in danger, and it is trying to scare your client with its smokescreen of intimidation because it fears that if the truth comes out, its days are numbered. Because OCD is, after all, just a paper tiger.

Thrill Seekers

There is a subgroup of people, sometimes referred to as "thrill seekers," who are essentially addicted to dangerous, heart-stopping activities. They are the people who ride the monster roller coasters over and over again, always trying to get into that first car of the coaster because the ride is the most intense from that vantage point. They are the ones who you see lifting their arms straight up rather than holding onto the locked bar across their chests because this way the ride becomes even more challenging.

Some thrill seekers go beyond this and regularly engage in sky diving, bungee jumping, hang gliding, or mountain climbing. These activities are usually seen by most of society as positive, in the sense that people are challenging themselves, building confidence, and building trust among the group members involved. We tend to admire people who engage in these activities, and for those of us who don't, we often secretly wish that we had the nerve to do the same. Advertising companies capitalize on this fantasy, which is why so many products are linked to high-risk sports in the ads that we see.

But not all thrill seekers look like this. Some are addicted to gambling or crime and get their thrills by avoiding loss or capture. Still, what they all have in common is that adrenaline-fueled "rush" of excitement when one brushes with danger or even possible death. This intense rush of adrenaline is something that most of us don't necessarily enjoy in very large amounts, though for sure we often seek it out in moderate amounts by engaging in activities that we find exciting. So what is it about these thrill seekers that make them different from most of the rest of us?

Thrill seekers have developed a different kind of emotional reaction to that release of high levels of adrenaline that create the intense rush. Most of us do not enjoy the feelings experienced at the high end of the adrenaline-surging continuum, and will seek to avoid those feelings whenever possible. It is these very feelings, however, that thrill seekers are addicted to. They have learned, usually through some kind of repeated exposure, to enjoy the high intensity physical reaction to extreme danger. They have immunized themselves through multiple exposures to varying challenges and are always looking for a newer, greater thrill. They enjoy the very thing that most of us would find too noxious to attempt, even if, in theory, we would like to engage in those activities. They have created an association between the experience of fear and the experience of pleasure.

This change in association, where a stimulus that once created only a negative emotional reaction now also creates a very positive one, or where the negative one is superseded by the positive one entirely, takes place quite regularly, even in the lives of those of us who would never consider ourselves thrill seekers. Things we dread often become the very things that we end up enjoying.

Things we dread often become the very things that we end up enjoying.

Let's look at my experience of learning how to play the piano for the first time as a middle-aged man. Every week my piano teacher would briefly review a piece of music and assign me the task of practicing it over the week, to be followed by my performing it for her at our next lesson. I hated this. I hated it because I had just sweated over learning the previous piece. I had gotten to a point where I could play that one relatively well, and was beginning to feel very positive about my accomplishment. And now, just when I was getting comfortable playing that piece, I had to start all over again with a new musical composition. I would look at the page of black circles and lines along the staffs of the new assignment, and the pattern would make no sense to me. I would have to teach myself how to read the music on the sheet as if I never knew anything about reading music, or so it felt. I very specifically remember that feeling of dread, when I sat down at my piano at home for the first time after being assigned a new piece, and feeling that pit in my stomach. It was only my overall desire to be able to play this instrument that kept me from quitting altogether during this period of my training.

But something interesting happened about ten months into my lessons. I had had so many experiences where those feelings of incompetence were replaced within just a week (all right, maybe sometimes within just a few weeks) with feelings of relative mastery, that I began to associate the stimuli of an unfamiliar piece of music with feelings of ultimate mastery and accomplishment. Part of me had the more natural and spontaneous reaction of dread that I had become familiar with, but it was almost as if, at the same time, I was looking forward to being able to reach that feeling of nirvana, that "rush" when the notes would finally all come together, and, without even being able to articulate how, I would find my hands responding to the notes on the page in just the right way. I soon found that, when I would open that new music assignment at home, and see those cryptic lines and circles, my reaction would be one of anticipation instead of dread. Fully expecting that I would be able to play the piece on the piano in just a few days while right now, in this moment, it was incomprehensible to me, was very exhilarating. It was as if I were saying to myself, "I can't do this *now*, but I *know* I will master it shortly!" I actually found myself reacting with a different set of emotions to a new piano piece. Each new challenge was now connected more with the rewarding experience of mastery, and less with the older experience of dread and frustration.

I expect that this learning experience must mirror that one in which the young child progresses beyond reading by sounding out letters, and instead, begins to "see" complete words. What power! What accomplishment! What a feeling of mastery! And as is always the case, the more difficult and overwhelming the original challenge, the sweeter and more exhilarating the celebration of mastery afterwards.

Although there are obvious differences between the activities reviewed earlier with regard to thrill seekers and that of learning a musical instrument, they do share this same dynamic. An event, a stimulus, previously experienced as negative, overwhelming, noxious, or uncomfortable actually becomes something that is enjoyed, that is desired.

The OCD Connection

This dynamic can be used in your OCD work with clients when introducing ERP. Many clients have reported that in the past they would simply avoid whatever triggered their OCD, always thinking first about how to "get around" the exposure situation, or how to minimize the actual exposure experience. They would find themselves automatically thinking about strategies to avoid or escape the discomfort of confronting an OCD-triggering stimuli. However, they report, later on as they progressed through treatment, they almost sought out opportunities to strengthen their recovery by looking for these very same stimuli. It was as if they had replaced the emotional reaction of fear and dread with one of the anticipation of mastery.

Once convinced of one's ability to overcome the challenge, and fully expecting to successfully negotiate the situation in such a way that one will ultimately not be bothered much by a particular triggering stimulus, it is easier to go forward with a positive association to the trigger and challenge oneself with exposure work. This of course makes the whole experience of exposure work move more quickly and lessens the pain of the experience. By discussing dynamics such as that illustrated in Thrill Seekers or in learning to play an instrument, you can introduce to clients the idea that their emotional reactions to ERP challenges may significantly change over time as they move away from focusing on the emotional discomfort these challenges produce and, instead, think of them more as opportunities to elicit feelings of mastery.

Fighting the Klingons

Star Trek has been in the collective consciousness of our popular culture for over four decades. Unlike many of today's science fiction films and TV shows, the Star Trek concept has always focused more on the characters and their relationships with each other and less on computer- generated and other special effects.

This is particularly true of the original TV series, not only because the show had a very tight budget, but because most of the effects seen in movies these days did not yet exist, as this series was aired in the mid- to late 1960s. Although the props and the "starships" of that original TV series were less than impressive, the messages communicated via the characters and the weekly plot of the show by far made up for any visual deficiencies. Race, religion, war, and politics were often dealt with in some way within the different storylines, which made the series more attractive to the thinking viewer.

For those not familiar with the series, Star Trek took place in the twenty-third century, at a time when war, disease, and inequality had ceased to exist throughout planet Earth, and the human race was engaged in such endeavors as exploring the universe. It was the particular mission of the USS Enterprise to "seek out new life and new civilizations," but while peace reigned on the home planet, there were still plenty of enemies out there in the vastness of space.

In the original series, the Federation of Planets were the "good guys" and included planet Earth as a member. The Federation stood for, well, more than anything else, the American way. One of the arch enemies of the Federation was the Klingon Empire. Given the political state in the real world at the time the TV show originally aired, the scripts were written such that the Klingon Empire often resembled the Soviet Union, and the struggle between the great two powers was not unlike the actual Cold War. The Federation and Klingon Empire were not actively engaged in open war, but whenever the two powers came into contact, there was often some kind of conflict, and sparks flew.

In one particular episode, the crew of the Enterprise find themselves face to face with a Klingon vessel. After a series of mishaps in which each side blames the other, the Klingon ship is destroyed, and a large part of its crew is transported over to the Enterprise. Both sides find themselves inexplicably stripped of their standard regulation weapons (phasers, which were essentially ray guns that could be set to stun or kill), and instead find themselves outfitted with weapons of a more primitive nature, such as swords or knives. Again, each captain blames the other, accusing him of being behind this strange set of affairs, although neither can come up with a plausible reason why the other would do such a thing.

Because they are stripped of the power to easily kill and destroy, the two sets of crew members struggle with each other on the Enterprise, chasing and stalking each other, and engaging blows in prolonged face-to-face conflict. This continues as the accusations fly from both sides until the answer makes itself evident. It appears that there is a third entity, another alien, which is responsible for the odd occurrences that have taken place.

This other alien species, it is finally determined, "lives off" of the emotional experience of hate between other life forms. This alien is depicted as nothing but a small spiral-like colored light that floats in, out, and around the ship. It has deliberately set up circumstances such that two mortal enemies would be forced to exist in close proximity, but would not be able to easily kill one another. Their hate would be ignited, and a sustained conflict would ensue, without the quick resolution of death.

Once the captains of both crews realize what has happened and for what reason and conclude that they cannot directly fight this third entity because it does not present itself as a physical being and does not have a spacecraft to attack, they each come to the same conclusion. They must stop the fighting immediately. The captains throw their swords down, awkwardly embrace each other while shouting out to the alien, "We will not fight on *your* terms! *We* decide who and when we shall fight! See? Now we are friends!" The episode ends with the alien life form leaving the ship and heading out into deep space, having given up on getting what it wanted from the Klingon and Federation crew members.

The OCD Connection

This is the defiant attitude taken by persons who want to maintain control of their own destinies, who resist enslavement by others, and who treasure their independence. In the world of OCD, the obsessions that flood a person's mind may be thought of as having been "sent" by the OCD in order to create a state of tension. This is similar to the alien force influencing conditions between the Federation and the Klingons so as to create a sense of tension between the two. As long as the two sides responded directly to their situation in a way that was most natural for them, that is, to fight each other, they actually "fed" the alien being, giving it exactly what it wanted. In the same way, as long as one engages in a compulsion in order to lower the degree of tension produced by an obsession, one also "feeds" the OCD. Like the alien force, we could say that OCD sends an obsession with the very hope that the person afflicted will respond with a compulsion, which ultimately strengthens the OCD. The alternative, of course, is to actively resist and challenge the OCD by not responding as expected, much as the Federation and the Klingons did. In so doing, you rob the OCD of the nourishment that it craves. Ultimately, like the alien force, it leaves the scene because its needs are not being met.

OCD sends an obsession with the very hope that the person afflicted will respond with a compulsion, which ultimately strengthens the OCD.

Fighting the Klingons can be used by therapists as yet another way of anthropomorphizing the OCD for clients, and as a vehicle for reframing ERP as an instrument of war against an enemy that is intent on domination.

5

When Symptoms Persist after Exposure

Exposure and response prevention (ERP) is not the perfect intervention. It helps tremendously a good deal of the time, but it is rare that a client will become completely asymptomatic toward the end of treatment, even when the appropriate application of ERP is employed and an effective medication regiment is followed. Typically, there are at least some residual symptoms or OCD-related difficulties that remain, even at a time when treatment termination is the appropriate clinical choice.

The stories in this chapter address concerns that clients might have as they struggle with accepting these residual symptoms even after having had a generally successful treatment experience that has resulted in a significant increase in functioning and quality of life. The therapist can share these stories as a way of helping clients to negotiate the chronic nature of the disorder, whilst maintaining a sense of personal accomplishment and empowerment.

The Three Waves

This next section is not a story in any sense of the word, but, rather, it describes a metaphor that represents the recovery arc through which OCD clients usually pass. The suggestion is that you as the therapist share it with clients utilizing some form of the following presentation:

"It is sometimes easy to miss the progress that has been made in your OC recovery program if you don't know where to look. Progress happens in different ways during different phases of treatment, and if you don't know what to expect, you may miss it, feel like you are wasting your time, and contemplate giving up."

In order to understand how OCD recovery progresses, it is first important to understand how the phases of OCD itself progress. OCD starts with an obsession, an intrusive thought that may seem to come out of nowhere, and over which you have no direct control. You are in effect the passive recipient of your obsession. You can think of this as the first wave in a series of waves that carry you through an obsessive-compulsive cycle. Think of this literally as a wave on the ocean that carries you through the first part of the OCD experience. A simple example might be to imagine that you are a father who experiences the thought, "If I pick up my baby and walk while carrying her, I might drop her and hurt or kill her!"

The second wave refers to your cognitive, emotional, and physiological reaction to the OCD obsession. It is what you say to yourself in response to hearing the obsession in your head and the consequent emotional reaction to what you say to yourself. In the example above, the obsession that you might drop your baby leads to your assessment that this is a reflection of reality and not just a symptom of your disorder, which consequently leads to the experience of anxiety. Your heart quickens, your muscles tighten, and your breathing becomes more pressured as your body reflects the experience of this heightened anxiety.

Immediately you may begin to think about ways of reducing this anxiety. You may think that you must put your child down immediately, that you need to enlist the assistance of someone else in order for her to be moved from one place to another, and, should you find yourself alone and responsible for her welfare, that you must immediately contact someone to come and help take care of her. Your anxiety escalates to panic, and you feel that you must do something *now*.

While the first wave is thrust upon you as if by some external force or internal demon, the second wave is an experience in which you play more of a direct role. You have processed your obsession in a certain way, and this has led to your emotional and physiological reaction. You may not be aware of it while you are in the middle of it, but you are in effect the creator of your response to your obsession, at some level processing the initial obsession, concluding that this is a real risk, that it is likely to happen, and that, in fact, your baby's death would be imminent should you pick her up and walk with her in your arms.

You may not be aware of it while you are in the middle of it, but you are in effect the creator of your response to your obsession.

This second wave leads to its natural conclusion in the third wave. If you believe that your child is in danger, if you believe that the longer you wait and do nothing to deal with this "danger" the greater the chances of you suffering the imagined negative consequences, then you will naturally seek to escape as soon as possible. In our example above, you will put your baby down, and you will contact someone else to help. You will avoid picking her up in the future and will avoid all situations in which you might find yourself alone and responsible for her.

The third wave is therefore your compulsion, your ritual. It is the execution of an observable behavior (although sometimes it is a purposeful, self-constructed thought) designed specifically to reduce the anxiety produced by the obsession. Even more than the second wave, this third wave is a direct result of your conscious will, your decision to engage in a particular activity with a specific goal in mind—to reduce the anxiety and avoid the feared consequence.

In summary, then, the three waves, in order of their occurrence, are (1) the experience of an intrusive obsession, followed by (2) cognitive processing of the obsession and the resulting experience of anxiety, ultimately resulting in (3) the execution of the compulsion. This is important to understand because recovery follows the same three waves, *but in the opposite direction.* Let us examine this more closely.

The OCD Connection

While we have been talking directly about OCD throughout this section, let us now explore what the implications of the Three Waves are for the treatment of this disorder. As the therapist, you can help your clients understand the progression of treatment via the utilization of the Three Waves metaphor.

As he begins to engage in fighting his OCD with ERP, your client first starts by changing his behavior. (When the ritual is a mental one, the thought then becomes the focus of the change, but we will not address that situation here.) However small the first steps may be, the focus is still on behavioral change more than anything else. In the example above, the father may hold the baby over the bed at higher and higher heights, start to walk with her around the house on carpeted floors, graduate to linoleum, then tile, and then move on to walking outside with her over concrete. He may start with his spouse standing right next to him when he carries the baby, then further away in the same room, then in another part of the house, and ultimately, with the father all alone in the house with his baby.

At every stage, the client starts by making a conscious choice to change his behavior. He is challenging the OCD at the third wave, and this is where the change first takes place. It is imperative to recognize, however, that when your client first begins his ERP experience, even though he may change his behavioral response and therefore eliminate the third wave of the OCD cycle, he should still expect that the first two waves will manifest themselves unchanged. The father in our example may still experience the obsession, "But I might drop and kill her!" and he may also experience a significant increase in anxiety as a result of hearing that thought in his head. He may still feel the physical symptoms that he has previously suffered. The first wave still triggers the second wave, but he has interrupted the process at the third wave, refusing to allow the thoughts and experience of anxiety to force him into engaging in the compulsion.

He can now do things that he was not able to do before, in this case, carry his child, even though he may continue to suffer with obsessions and the resultant anxiety. Not yet recovered from his OCD experience, he is not where he was before. He has more behavioral control. He has more freedom.

Because of the process of desensitization and habituation (see the Horror Movie story), it is just a matter of time before the repeated exposure of carrying his baby around results in a reduction of the anxiety experienced. This is manifested by the reduction of the physiological experience of anxiety; that is, his breathing and heart rate will return to more normal levels, as will his muscle tension and other anxiety symptoms.

At this point he has interrupted the OCD cycle at both the third and the second waves. He may still be plagued by the worry-thought, "I might drop and kill my baby!" but he is more easily able to identify this as an OCD thought, as a symptom of his disorder, and not representative of a real threat. He experiences little, if any anxiety, and he is no longer engaging in his compulsive ritual.

There are a good number of OCD clients who make it to this point in recovery, and feel as if they have not gotten over their problem. This is not entirely true, and it would be a mistake to assume that treatment was a failure. In actuality the person is no longer engaging in a compulsive ritual; in our example above, the father is not avoiding carrying his baby. In addition he does not experience undo stress, although some residual anxiety might still exist. So, again in our illustration, he may be able to carry the baby while at the same time feeling very little or no anxiety, but he may still be plagued by these intrusive thoughts or images which communicate the idea that he *might* drop the baby. He is able to label those thoughts as OCD thoughts, and may be able to dismiss them out of hand, but the intrusive thoughts still exist.

For many clients, and for many differing OC symptom presentations, the obsession itself does indeed seem to fade and even disappear completely after a period of time. The OCD is essentially silenced, and the client no longer experiences the OCD cycle, at least not in relation to this particular circumstance. The client has successfully overcome his OCD experience in such a situation.

The point to be made here by the therapist is that recovery happens in the opposite direction of the natural progression of the OCD cycle. One begins recovery by focusing on the third wave, the compulsion, because that is where there is the most direct influence, that is where the person has the most power to change. Recovery then moves towards the reduction and even elimination of anxiety through the process of desensitization/habituation. The person's assessment of his obsession changes as well, as he is able to better label the experience as nothing more than an OCD symptom. Once these steps have successfully been negotiated, than more likely than not, the obsession itself will begin to fade as a natural result of the elimination of the two other waves.

Recovery happens in the opposite direction of the natural progression of the OCD cycle.

Clients will sometimes come into therapy complaining that they have been working very hard but have not made much progress. They may state that they still have worrisome thoughts and still experience anxiety, but they may miss the importance of the fact that they are now not letting the OCD control their behavior through compulsions. Alternatively, other clients may complain that whereas they have complete behavioral control and can do everything that their OCD had not permitted in the past, and although they now experience mild or no anxiety around the particular issue that they have been working on, they still are plagued by the intrusive thoughts.

Although this may be frustrating and unpleasant, of course, it is by no means the same as not having behavioral freedom, or feeling trapped in a perpetual state of fear.

By utilizing the image of the three waves, you, as therapist, can better illustrate to those who might feel that progress has eluded them that they are making an error in their evaluation. You can use the Three Waves to demonstrate that progress has indeed been made, even though some aspects of the disorder continue to exist.

A Fly in the Room

There are several approaches to dealing with the problem of obsessions.

Engaging in the compulsion. The client can, of course engage in the compulsion, assuming there is one connected to it. If the obsession is, "Maybe I just hit someone with my car when I turned that last corner!" she can simply turn her car around, drive back, and check to make sure that there are no bodies and there is no blood. This will help her to relieve the anxiety associated with the obsession (most of the time, but not always—after all, she could have hit that person so hard that she sent him airborn, flying into the bushes, and now she has to get out of the car and visually inspect the underbrush), but ultimately, she pays the price by feeding the OCD. Even if she responds to residual anxiety by continuing to engage in further checking compulsions in order to allay her fears, by say watching the local news or reading the local newspapers for reports on hit-and-run accidents, or inspecting the front of her car for blood, she can count on the fact that the obsession will return again, next time with even more persuasive power.

Distraction. An alternative is for the client to distract himself from the obsession and attempt to ignore it, trying not to focus on it at all. He may engage in another behavior to take his mind off of the obsession and try to forget about it. This works pretty well, *if* he can do this. Most of the time, for most obsessions, people with OCD cannot.

Rational analysis. Here the attempt is to rationally argue with the obsession in an attempt to have it dissipate. In the above example, the conversation that the client would try to initiate with himself would go something like, "Look, I'm sure if I hit someone I would have felt a thud, and that I would have noticed the thud, even if I was not really paying that close attention to the road those few moments back there. It's pretty well lit outside and, even though I passed a few people, most everyone was a good distance from the car, even the few people who were walking along in the street. Anyway, I *always* think that I hit somebody, and it never turns out that I did, so chances are I didn't this time as well."

This strategy of "cognitive restructuring," which works so well with other forms of anxiety such as phobias and panic, usually ends up failing short with OCD, especially used in the way illustrated above. Although cognitive restructuring tends to work well under certain circumstances, it will often fail as a direct challenge to OCD obsessions. This is true especially if it is used in isolation and without applying other techniques. This is because OCD doesn't function on logic. In fact the energy that the client spends trying to fight his way out of an obsession in this way usually serves to strengthen the OCD itself rather than help the client to feel much better about anything. This is the most popular intervention that other people use when they see a person with OCD struggling with an obsession. The attempt to rationally talk the person "out of the obsession" rarely if ever works.

Exposure and response prevention. Anyone who knows anything about the appropriate use of behavior therapy for OCD knows that ERP is the behavioral treatment of choice for OCD. Many of the other stories in this book address the specifics of this approach, so let's move on.

Medication. Since the prevailing sentiment is that OCD is best treated by a combination of ERP and medication, this, too, has a role in many OCD cases. But let's turn to the point of this story, which is to highlight yet another alternative: *acceptance.*

Here is the relevant story. Arielle is sitting in a room reading a book. In the middle of reading, she gets distracted by a fly that flies a few inches away from her head. She hears the buzz, give a little "shoo" movement with her hand, and it is gone. But a few moments later it returns, and she has to shoo it away again.

After a few more repetitions of these interruptions, she gets frustrated and decides to put her book aside. She declares war on the fly and seeks it out with her fly swatter. She sees it has landed on the very tip of a pencil that is standing in her pencil cup that holds an arrangement of other pencils, pens, and markers. She goes after the fly with her swatter, but misses and sends the pencil cup and all the writing implements that it was holding flying all over the room.

The fly buzzes around the room a few times, and then gently lands on the top of a large stack of CDs in their cases that are piled high on the corner of her desk. She strikes, the fly flies out from under her swatter, and she is left with a floor covered in CDs and their broken cases.

The pursuit continues with the same negative results. Her computer monitor, her collection of small glass figurines, her favorite flower vase, the table lamp—they all end up broken on the floor while she sits there, swatter in hand, as that obnoxious fly buzzes around her head.

The story can go on like this indefinitely, with Arielle chasing after the fly, destroying everything in her path, and never getting to her book. Or, she can do something completely different. She can come to a point where she accepts that the fly is there, and will stay there, flying around the room and even coming fairly close to her every now and then. But she can choose to read her book anyway and let the fly alone. By accepting that she is not going to eliminate the fly, at the very least, she stops breaking things, and gets most of her reading done. She may even get to the point where she learns to ignore the fly, hardly noticing it at all, thereby minimizing its disruptive effects. But even if she can't ignore it, by letting go of her need to obliterate the cause of her annoyance, it ends up exercising less power over her.

The OCD Connection

By letting go of her need to obliterate the cause of her annoyance, it ends up exercising less power over her.

This technique of acceptance is a particularly important therapeutic option when dealing with atypical obsessions, where there are no easily identified specific compulsions that need to be done. These are sometimes called "pure" obsessions, but the existence of obsessions without compulsions is under dispute in the clinical community, and some believe that often the compulsions are there, just less obvious.

Sometimes the client's obsessions can be vague and unclear, such as an obsession that something is just not "right," or that the meaning of an experience is questionable ("Am I really happy? What does this experience really mean in my life?") Such obsessions have no observable, distinct compulsions to eliminate them and are difficult to confront cognitively. Even ERP becomes a tricky intervention to use here, since these are not defined obsessions, they are more like "shadows" of obsessions, and their lack of definition makes the development of a specific ERP intervention difficult. Acceptance therapy for these obsessions, therefore, becomes the treatment of choice.

When obsessions present as rhetorical questions that have no real answer (e.g., "Is that thing really beautiful? What is beauty, anyway?"), the treatment of choice is to label the thoughts as OCD thoughts and to accept that they cannot be eliminated directly. The therapist can help such OCD clients by reminding them that they do not need to "resolve" these thoughts or eliminate the uncertainty created by them, as they are but merely words in the mind spoken by the OCD. By accepting the obsessions as the part of the illness over which they have no direct control, the impact and interference tend to be minimal. It is about letting the fly live and focusing instead on reading your book to the best of your ability.

Vinyl Albums

Old enough to remember vinyl albums? I mean really remember *using* them, when you had no choice, before the iPod? Before CDs? The beauty of the art on the album cover, the thickness of the big black disc, the sheer *size* of it all made for a full experience that went beyond merely listening to the music! You couldn't fit one of *those* things so easily in your purse or pocket!

The image of vinyl records triggers for me the memory of one year, long ago, when I was at sleep-away camp. Someone had brought an old record player to camp, the kind with the 6-inch speaker, where you had to place the arm with the needle in it onto the record disk by yourself, rather than push a button and have it guide itself onto the disc automatically (the robotic needle arm became more prominent by the mid-1970s). One of my bunkmates placed an album on the record player and put the lights out in the bunk just as we all went to bed for the night. It was a recording of a yoga/relaxation exercise presentation, and the entire record was the sound of a man talking gently, guiding us through the relaxation exercise.

As I lay there in bed in the dark, listening to the record, I found myself wanting to delve into the deep state of relaxation being described but found myself incredibly distracted by the hisses and pops. To those of you who might have limited experience with record albums, allow me to explain the various imperfections that we used to hear in album recordings.

Compared to CDs, albums were significantly more vulnerable to scratches if mishandled. When an album had multiple surface scratches, this resulted in a relatively consistent "hissing" sound heard in the background of the recording and little popping or ticking sounds that were punctuated throughout the album. That was the case with this particular record, and I found myself annoyed at this distraction, which made it hard to follow the relaxation instructions and reap the benefits of the exercise.

A few minutes into it, however, the narrator introduced the idea of incorporating distractions into the relaxation exercise itself. "There may be sounds around you that you might hear," he stated. "Allow them to flow through you and out of you, and make them part of your relaxation experience." He gave several examples of what he meant, but one in particular was relevant to me. "If you notice, for instance," he went on to say, "that the album that you are listening to is scratched, and you hear hissing and popping sounds, just imagine that you are listening to this record in a room with a crackling fireplace, and that these sounds are coming from the wood being consumed by the fire. The sounds then serve to elevate your state of relaxation and enhance your experience. They become part of the picture, rather than detracting from it."

How right he was! Immediately, I shifted into a much deeper state of relaxation, embracing the sounds, and making them part of my experience. I can't remember what happened next—I had fallen fast asleep!

Turning the record scratches into an asset rather than a liability would be termed "reframing" by many psychologists. Literally, it means putting another frame around a picture, to make the picture look different, usually better in some way. Reframing essentially means changing the meaning of any thought, behavior, or experience in such a way so that it becomes more positive rather than negative.

Reframing essentially means changing the meaning of any thought, behavior, or experience in such a way so that it becomes more positive rather than negative.

The OCD Connection

Reframing has an important place in the treatment of OCD. Often, a person who goes through successful treatment may find that the symptoms are finally under control but that a certain amount of obsessing continues. The "hissing and pops," so to speak, in the person's mind can be dealt with in different ways. If seen as an intolerable annoyance or symbolic representations of the OCD that must be eradicated, then much energy is spent focusing on their complete elimination, draining energy from more positive pursuits. This usually leads to frustration and, to some degree, depression, since for many people the complete elimination of these obsessions remains elusive.

If, on the other hand, the client, with your assistance, can accept these obsessions as the vestiges of a foe basically conquered, then they take on a whole new meaning. They become the cries of the vanquished king, whose armies you have destroyed, whose villages you have conquered, but who must, like an aging lion, hear himself roar in a feeble attempt to convince himself and everyone else that he still poses a threat. But the client knows better. It is merely the shadow of a slain enemy, the trophy that reminds your client every day that while the enemy still lives, the client is the victor and now rules the kingdom.

Train in the Backyard

A co-worker invites you and your spouse over to her home for dinner with her family for the very first time. She lives in a very attractive neighborhood, and her house and backyard are likewise very appealing but with one exception. She lives right next to the tracks of a major railroad line. Her property line literally goes right up to a chain link fence, and just on the other side of the fence lie the tracks.

You are all sitting at the dining room table. It is late spring, and the windows, which face the backyard, are wide open. Somewhere between the main course and dessert, a train comes rolling by. The whole house shakes. You can hear the crystal vibrating in the china cabinet, you can see the water shaking in your water goblet, and you can feel the vibrations running through the floor boards and into your feet as well as through the chair in which you are seated, vibrating your entire body. It is *very* loud.

You are in the middle of a conversation with your co-worker's spouse, and when the train runs by, the spouse, who had been talking to you from across the table, talks much more loudly, almost as if he were yelling, to finish his point. Other than this adjustment, there is no change whatsoever in the family's behavior. The kids continue eating, your co-worker passes one of the serving platters to your spouse, and no one seems to react at all to this major intrusion. You look at your spouse, eyes blazing with surprise, as if to say, "Can you believe this?" and she looks right back at you, with an expression conveying a combination of shock, surprise, and amusement.

You are very shaken up. You are taken by surprise at the intensity of the train rushing past and are essentially speechless for what must be at least thirty seconds after the train has gone by.

"Does that happen often?" you finally asked the family. Your co-worker looks at you with a confused expression, and then, slowly, reveals a slight, embarrassed smile. To your astonishment, she says,

"Oh, did the train just pass?" You look around the table and can see that her entire family is likewise seemingly oblivious to what had just happened.

"You mean you didn't hear it?" you ask, incredulously.

"I guess I did," comes the answer, "but we've just learned not to pay attention to it."

Not pay attention to it?! How in the world could they not pay attention to it?! Further questioning reveals that, while your co-worker and her family members had actually been aware that the train had indeed passed, they were not truly conscious of it. If asked, "Did a train go by the house while you were eating dinner?" they would have each most likely responded, "I think so."

This is reminiscent of the experience of "highway hypnosis," with which most people are familiar. If you drive to work every day, always taking the same route, you might have some recollection of some of the things you passed along the way, but you would not truly remember turning at a particular traffic light or stopping at a particular stop sign. You are aware at some level of the journey to work, but on another level you are essentially on "automatic," having tuned out the experience as a result of familiarity.

Your co-worker and her family have essentially unwittingly utilized the same adjustment technique. They have learned to "tune out" even this very disruptive event of a train rushing by their home, an event that stimulated the senses of sight and touch as well as the obvious one of sound. They even had adjusted their behavior, in particular the spouse raising his voice to accommodate the noise, and yet still were apparently unaware of the train passing by. It is truly amazing the degree to which people can accommodate to disturbances if they are exposed to them enough repeatedly over a long period of time.

The OCD Connection

It is truly amazing the degree to which people can accommodate to disturbances if they are exposed to them enough repeatedly over a long period of time.

When clients find themselves at a point in treatment where they have worked hard at exposure therapy and have found that they can successfully control their behavioral compulsions, but they find that the obsessions, to some degree, continue, it is good for them to hear this story. There is sometimes the experience of frustration, or even depression, as a result of the realization that even if they can prevent themselves from engaging in washing, checking, or some other compulsive behavior, their obsessive thoughts might continue indefinitely, and might even be omnipresent.

It is important to note that as a matter of course this is not always what happens during ERP treatment. Very often, a reduction or cessation in behavioral compulsions will be followed by an actual reduction in the experience of obsessions; sometimes even the entire elimination of them. But in many cases, the obsessions persist. And it is here where the person with OCD becomes frustrated.

When this occurs it is important to encourage your clients with the knowledge that, as they continue to refrain from their compulsive behaviors, their obsessions may also continue to weaken and become less frequent. But even if this does not occur, you can let them know that with time, they will most likely learn to better ignore the "OCD Train" as it passes through their minds. Even if it is not just background noise, even if it makes for significant racket, it need not detract from the experiences in which they are engaged, it need not interrupt the activities with which they are involved.

Sometimes it seems as though people can and do get used to just about anything. People not noticing a train passing by their backyard as they sit less that 100 feet away at their dining room table illustrates the extent to which this is true and thus serves as an excellent story to share with your clients under these conditions.

6

When a Child Has OCD

The following set of stories are geared to families with younger children who are diagnosed with OCD. Several of these stories are aimed directly at the parents as part of their psychoeducation and as a prelude to their needing both to make behavioral changes in themselves and to learn some basic OCD treatment concepts that they can then reinforce in the home between scheduled appointments with their child's therapist.

Ready for Takeoff

If you have ever traveled by plane, you have experienced the brief safety instructional and general information presentation given either in person or via video recording by one of the flight attendants before takeoff. Things like noting where the exits are ("and don't forget that the closest one might be behind you!"), reviewing how to operate the life vest, and explaining the need to pay attention when the "buckle your seatbelt" sign is illuminated are some of the important pieces of information reviewed.

Another such piece of information always reviewed during these presentations involves those oxygen masks that are supposed to drop down out of the compartment above your head during an emergency. Passengers are specifically instructed on how to place these masks on, and then the flight attendant makes a special announcement to those traveling with persons who may require assistance with the masks. These particular passengers are instructed that, in the event of an emergency, one should put the oxygen mask on oneself first, and only then assist the person requiring help. These instructions make sense because if you spend too much time assisting the other person first, you may end up passing out from lack of oxygen, and then you are not only in danger yourself but you are no longer in a position to help the person requiring assistance.

Although these instructions may pertain to someone traveling with an elderly or ill person, most of the time this situation arises when one is traveling with a child. It is easy to imagine a situation where, panicked by the state of emergency taking place on a flying aircraft, parents would focus only on getting that potentially life-saving mask on their children first and not give any thought about getting the masks on themselves until they were sure that their children were safely fitted with the device. But, for the reasons reviewed above, that would be a mistake. In order for parents to protect their children most effectively, they must first make sure that they themselves are out of harm's way.

The OCD Connection

In order for parents to protect their children most effectively, they must first make sure that they themselves are out of harm's way.

When parents bring their children with OCD in for treatment, they have a very specific agenda: "Make my child well." When they learn that in cognitive behavioral therapy the style of treatment is not so much that the therapist does anything "to" the client, but instead the therapist instructs the client in the ways she can help herself, parents then want the therapist to tell them and their children what their children need to do differently in order to get better. These parents are sometimes caught off guard when they learn that the first step in this kind of situation, at least a good deal of the time, is not about having the child do anything differently at all, but about having the *parents* do something differently.

As is the case with alcohol and drugs, OCD can become a family affair. Family members, especially parents, can become wrapped up in their child's OCD demands. In an attempt to protect their child from the emotional discomfort of the obsession, parents will assist their child in performing a compulsive ritual, or even do that ritual for them, or play a specific role in the carrying out that ritual. Although this serves the purpose of temporarily reducing the anxiety and emotional discomfort of the child, it ultimately serves the OCD, because giving into the OCD by performing rituals to decrease anxiety will always result in the strengthening of the obsessions. This, in turn, often leads to the requirement of more lengthy, complicated, and/or bizarre ritualistic behaviors.

A child might ask a parent to check in the closet of the child's room to make sure there are no monsters in there. Whereas complying to this request serves the healthy function of reassurance on the part of the parent and leads to diminished anxiety on the part of a child under *normal* circumstances, this is *not* the case when OCD enters the picture. With OCD such checking on the part of the parent will inevitably lead to requests (or demands) for more elaborate checking or other such behaviors. Parents might soon find that they are requested by their child to now look in between each piece of clothing hanging in the closet or might have demands made that they must now recite a particular script such as "I see no monsters in Mary's closet." This occurs because the initial reassurance serves to strengthen the OCD symptoms, creating the need for these more elaborate rituals on the part of the parent.

And so in therapy, rather than having the *child* make changes in her requests or demands of her parents, we often start by negotiating with the child as to how the *parents* will be changing their responses to those demands and requests. Before the therapy can more directly address the OCD cycle of obsessions and compulsions in the child, the parents must first be assisted in extricating themselves from the cycle, and that means changing their behavioral response to the OCD demands.

In this way, the parent is no longer under the direct influence of the OCD and has in effect modeled for the child the concept of fighting back, not giving into OCD demands, and standing your ground. Once the parent has removed OCD from directly controlling her own behaviors, just as the parent on the airplane who has secured her own oxygen mask and is now safely able to assist her child in putting on the child's mask, the mother of the child with OCD is now in a more healthy position to assist her child in learning and employing the techniques for combating OCD.

Getting a Medical Diagnosis

There are times when you might have had a series of physical symptoms and were confused as to what exactly was the problem. Especially if the symptoms were severe or unusual, this set of circumstances might be frightening, and you could find yourself asking, "What in the world is *wrong* with me?" Most of the time, a trip to the doctor under such circumstances will result in an immediate reduction of this confusion and anxiety as the physician provides you with a diagnosis.

Even before you take your first dose of medicine, before you start your physical therapy, or even before you prepare for a needed operation, there is a certain relief in knowing that *at least you now know* what is wrong and can begin to take steps to make things right again. There is a sense that those professionals who are helping you now have a specific plan of action in mind, a protocol that they will be following for you, in order to nurse you back to health.

In addition, providing a diagnosis is a way of giving a name to your illness, which is a good way to separate yourself *from* that illness. There is "you" and then there is your illness—the thing that has attached itself to you and that has now somehow been interfering with your functioning or has changed the way you experience the world in some way. Giving your illness a name is a good way to help give you a sense of control over that illness. You can now harness your energies against the illness, do specific things that target it, and work on eliminating it.

The OCD Connection

This dynamic exists as well for psychiatric illnesses, and specifically it is very true for those persons suffering with OCD. But the importance of labeling one's OCD is even greater in those cases when the person with OCD is a child. By the very nature of their size and place in our society, children often do not feel in control of their world. Most things are dictated to them, and everyone else is usually much bigger and stronger than they are and has authority over them. This, of course, is how it should be since they are, after all, children, but these circumstances do create a certain degree of tension and frustration at times. This may lead to the tantrums that we see in small children, who are tired of always being told what, how, and when to do things and ultimately demand to do something "*my* way!"

Other consequences of these circumstances are attempts to experience some sense of control by becoming "obsessive compulsive" and ritualistic about certain things. For example, the stuffed animals need to be lined up in a very specific order before bedtime, the peas cannot touch the mashed potatoes on the dinner plate, or if they do, they cannot be eaten, and so on. This does not constitute OCD but, rather, reflects normal developmental coping strategies. But such age-appropriate behaviour patterns illustrate the fact that children strive for a sense of mastery and control in their lives.

When children struggle with symptoms of OCD but have not yet been diagnosed, they will often find themselves getting into a lot of trouble.

When children struggle with symptoms of OCD but have not yet been diagnosed, they will often find themselves getting into a lot of trouble. Everyone around them, their parents, siblings, teachers, and even friends, are frustrated with them, or are even angry with them. Parents or teachers might punish them for "misbehaving" or for not following instructions, or for breaking the rules. Siblings and friends may make fun of them or yell at them because of their "stupid" behaviors. This of course results in the child feeling many of the things that children in general already feel—frustrated, out of control, and powerless, but even more so. In addition, they often feel that they are just "being bad." This can result in their becoming depressed, withdrawn, and feeling confused and alone. They may feel misunderstood by everyone around them and even find that they themselves do not understand their own thoughts and behaviors. They may believe that they are stupid, crazy, or the only person in the world who is going through these kinds of experiences.

Labeling the OCD through diagnosis serves to put everything in perspective. It is about understanding that there is you, and then there is your OCD, the "thing" that is responsible for the problems you have been experiencing. Adults can more easily grasp this concept, and so to help children with this, we suggest that they not only label their symptoms as OCD, but also that they actually give the OCD a name. "Mr. Pushy," "Ms. Meany," "Blueblob," "Oscar," the list goes on and on. It helps them to feel that it isn't so much that they are bad, even if they have not been following the rules set by adults, but that they have been, in some way, manipulated by Mr. OCD. It is *he* who is bad. Then, rather than the conflict being defined as parents, teachers, and others on one side, and the child alone on the other, it is a conflict where everybody, including the child, is on one side, and Mr. OCD is alone, on the other. Everyone can now work together to defeat Mr. OCD.

This labeling process goes a long way to help assuage the guilt children often feel about their OCD behaviors. Since in labeling the OCD they now know what they are fighting, it helps children to feel more hopeful that there may be something that can be done to regain control, and this realization may in turn serves to reduce their experience of depression. Labeling the OCD in this manner also helps parents direct their anger at the OCD and not at their child who is struggling and suffering with a psychiatric disorder. For both parents and child, it helps them to feel that now there is an understanding of the relationship between the sometimes myriad of strange and at times bizarre thoughts and the ritualistic behaviors, which follow these thoughts. And if they have access to good information and appropriate therapy, there is now a sense of the availability of interventions, tools and techniques, a direction that one can move toward in order to achieve recovery, as well as a sense of greater support from a community with other children and families, who likewise have been afflicted by this disorder.

Mr. OCD is not an excuse for the child to not work on getting better. This is not about the child engaging in a ritual or some avoidance behavior all the while saying, "It's not my fault! Mr. OCD did it!"

"While it may be," we might say to the child, "that you did not ask for this and that this thing has been controlling you, you now know what this "thing" is. You now know the skills that you need to employ in order to weaken Mr. OCD's control over you, to break free, and to be the master of yourself."

Labeling OCD and anthropomorphizing it, giving it "life," giving it a name, drawing a picture of it, and talking about "him" as if he existed as separate from the child, serves to demystify and depathologize the experience of OCD. It provides direction and focus, hope and empowerment, and, even if nothing yet about the child's obsessions and compulsions have changed, everything is already different. Parents can be helped to understand the importance of the strategy of naming the OCD when told the story of diagnosing a medical illness. The story tends to reflect a common sentiment, and "brings home" the experience of centering that labeling of an illness provides for many, allowing the parents to take seriously this seemingly "silly," or "childish" clinical intervention.

Bully in the Playground

Ralph is in the fifth grade. He is eleven years old. He is a nice kid and a good student, but Ralph is shy and is thin and smaller than most of his classmates. He does not have too many friends.

Ralph has a problem. Ralph's problem is Max. Max is a problem because he is a bully, and he picks on Ralph all the time. In the classroom, Max tells Ralph that if he doesn't give him the answers to the homework questions, he will beat him up after school. In the lunchroom, Max tells Ralph that he needs to give him his lunch money, or he'll stick Ralph's head in the toilet the next time he catches him in the bathroom. He tells Ralph that he needs to let him go in front of him in the cafeteria line or he'll take his nice sweater from him. When Ralph is at home online on the computer, Max threatens to break his glasses if Ralph doesn't write the book summary for him that is due tomorrow.

Ralph has tried everything to make Max happy so that Max will leave him alone. Ralph brings extra lunch money to school so that he has some money for himself and some money that he can give to Max when it is demanded of him. He runs to get on the cafeteria line early, so he can get a good spot to give to Max, because Max gets angry if Ralph gets him a spot too far in the back of the line. Ralph will often prepare a second page of answers to homework questions just to have ready to give to Max when he asks for it; sometimes he even stays up later on school nights in order to write a second homework paper when Max tells him to.

But Ralph is finding that his strategy of placating Max is not helping his situation. In fact, things are getting worse. Max is always asking for more and more things of Ralph, always threatening him. And Ralph is always in a state of fear. If he hasn't prepared an extra homework, he tries very hard to avoid Max in class. Sometimes he doesn't go to the bathroom all day for fear that Max may find him in there and get to him. If he forgets extra lunch money, he avoids the cafeteria altogether for fear of dealing with Max. There are always more things that Ralph has to do for Max, more things to remember, more things to look out for, more things to worry about. It's a miracle that Ralph is even able to learn in school at all. And sometimes he doesn't, because sometimes he is just so tired of dealing with Max that he makes believe his is physically ill, and he stays home from school just to take a break from all the stress.

Sandra, one of Ralph's few friends, sees what has been going on for a long time now. She tries to help Ralph. "Ralph, tell your Mom! Tell your teacher!" But Ralph is afraid. Max has told him that if he tells anyone, if he does anything to try to stop Max from controlling him, that Max will make things even worse for him. And so nothing changes.

David, who sits next to Ralph in class and lives on his block, also tries to encourage Ralph. "Ralph! You gotta fight him! You gotta tell him to get off your back! Tell him you won't do the things he asks—punch him in the nose if you have to!"

But Ralph won't consider it—"Max is much bigger than me, and he will beat me up! He will break my glasses and steal my sweater," says Ralph.

One day Ralph is in the school playground on one of the swings. Sandra is swinging with him, laughing and talking. He had just won a pin in English class that day for writing the best composition in the class, and he was wearing the pin proudly on his shirt as he swung up and down. It was a good day. It was one of those few times that he hadn't noticed Max around, and he was feeling pretty good and free of his problems. All of a sudden, Max appears. Ralph catches his eye as Max motions for Ralph to get off the swing and come on over to him.

"Don't go!" Sandra whispers to him as she notices what is going on. "Stay here on the swings with me! Don't let him boss you around!" But that seems too difficult, too scary for Ralph. He stops the swing and sheepishly walks over to Max.

It is in the corner of the playground, and there are plenty of kids—but not a teacher in sight. Ralph's heart quickens, and he begins to feel a sick feeling in his stomach as he approaches Max. "I want you to pull down your pants" says Max.

"What?" cries Ralph.

"Pull down your pants. Right here, right now. In front of everyone, so that they can see your underpants!" Ralph was caught off guard. This was something new and different. Something Max had never demanded before. And for no reason that Ralph could think of. Ralph looks around. Sandra is standing in front of the swings, watching from a distance. Other kids have also stopped playing ball, and a couple have stopped sliding down the slide and are just standing there watching him and Max.

Ralph's mind starts to race. "What do I do? What do I do?!" he asks himself. "If I do what he says, it'll be *so* embarrassing! How will I ever be able to show my face in school again!" He panics. "But if I don't do what he says, who knows *what* he'll do to me!" These thoughts race through Ralph's mind at lightening speed. But then he finds himself thinking, "But if I do as he says, what will he ask of me next? This will never stop! I can't take it anymore!" Ralph swallows hard. He takes a deep breath. "NO!" he shouts.

Suddenly things seem very quiet. Ralph sees Sandra out of the corner of his eye. Her face has a strange expression that looks like a combination of shock and glee. The kids who stopped sliding and playing ball stand there with their eyes fixed on Ralph and their mouths open. Ralph waits for what seems like an eternity to see what Max will do.

"Why, you little ..." says Max as he reaches over to grab Ralph, but Ralph is quick and jumps out of the way. "Hey!" yells Max, again reaching out with his other arm, this time with his hand in the shape of a fist headed right toward Ralph's shoulder. But Ralph again backs out of harm's way, and Max's arm flies through thin air, throwing him off balance and causing him to fall to the ground. Everyone watching laughs out loud, and in that moment Ralph scans the crowd of faces and smiles, feeling something he doesn't remember ever feeling before, or at least, not for a really long time. He feels strong. He feels courageous. He feels free!

He feels strong. He feels courageous. He feels free!

This moment of bliss is interrupted by the sight of Max, now really angry because he has been embarrassed by the fall, straightening himself up in front of Ralph, standing a full foot taller than he is, with big wide shoulders, dirtied from having fallen face down on the ground. "Run!" cries Sandra, and with her voice echoing in his ears, Ralph takes off, with Max in hot pursuit.

"I'll git' you!" cries Max, closing in on Ralph as they both circle around the swing set. Max tackles him at the ankles, and Ralph goes down hard.

Max turns Ralph around so that he is lying on his back. "Give me that stupid pin!" he yells at Ralph.

"No!" comes the response, even louder than the first time. They struggle, each with his hands on the pin, and then Ralph loosens it, detaches it from his shirt, and purposely throws it over the gate so that it falls outside of the playground. "If you want it, go get it yourself!" Max is stunned by this unexpected response from Ralph. He is not exactly sure himself what he should do.

Max again winds up to take a punch at Ralph. Ralph grabs his arm with both of his hands and with all his might pushes it out of the way. They struggle on the ground for a minute or so, and during this time

Max punches Ralph a couple of times in the arm. Then the school bell rings, and the boys separate without saying another word. As he heads back to the school building, Sandra runs up and joins Ralph. "Are you OK?" she asks him.

"Yeah," he answers, "My arm hurts where he hit me, but I'm fine."

Ralph was more than fine. He had stood up to Max. He had said "No" to him for the very first time. And even though he lost his pin and his arm hurt, and he was not sure what Max might try to do to him next time they met, he didn't really care. This was a small price to pay for feeling as good as he felt right now. And it sure felt better than what he imagined it would have felt like had he pulled his pants down in the middle of the playground.

The next day, Ralph stands on the cafeteria line, waiting for Max. He has a really good spot toward the front of the line, and it is pizza day, which is always everyone's favorite. Max enters the cafeteria on the other side of the room, and begins to walk toward the lunch line. Ralph waits for Max to see him. When he finally sees Ralph standing on line saving a spot for him, Max smiles an evil smile, as if to say, "I'm still the boss!" When Max is about twenty feet from the line, Ralph, with a stern look directly at Max, walks right out of that line and sits down at one of the tables next to Sandra, who has already gotten pizza for the two of them. Max has to go to the end of the line.

When Max whispers to Ralph that he needed one of the quiz answers during science class, Ralph ignores him. When Max IMs him at night on his computer, Ralph ignores him at first, and then blocks his e-mail address. Ralph is feeling really proud about standing up to Max in all these ways but is really still kind of scared about what he is doing. He keeps thinking that he will pay a terrible price somewhere down the line for being so gutsy. And then the day comes.

One day, in the boy's bathroom, Max steps out of one of the bathroom stalls when Ralph is there at one of the sinks. "So, you think you're a big shot now, eh?" says Max. Ralph steals a quick glance at the door leading out of the bathroom. Max steps in front of it. "Don't even *think* about running this time!" he says. Max grabs him by the shoulders, and they both struggle as Max pushes Ralph into one of the stalls, forcing him to his knees and pushing his head toward the open toilet bowl.

Ralph's head is in the bowl, but just as his hair is about to touch the water, he screams out a loud "Ahhh!" and in an attempt to push away from the toilet, pulls his elbow sharply back, thrusting it into Max's ribs, pushing him back up against the wall of the bathroom stall. Max sits on the floor of the stall and moans, and Ralph stands up over him. Ralph, realizes what he has done, and waits a long minute. "Enough!" he shouts at Max. "It's over!"

From that day on, Max no longer bothered Ralph. Ralph could go to the boy's bathroom without looking over his shoulder, could walk into the cafeteria without scanning ahead to see if Max was around, could turn on his computer at home without a feeling of dread that Max would IM him. He was free, and he felt strong. He felt good about himself, and he found he liked himself better. There were other bullies in school of course, not just Max, but whenever anyone tried to push Ralph around, or tried to threaten him in any way, Ralph stood his ground. He found that by standing up to bullies, they tend to back off, because you are not an easy target. Ralph had learned a lot.

The OCD Connection

The story of Ralph and Max can be told directly to children. It often helps to have parents in the office as well, so they can also hear the story and can then reinforce its lessons at home. Your instructions to the child in your office could then continue directly in the following manner:

"Your OCD is like a bully as well. It tells you that you better do certain things or it will make your life miserable. It threatens you. It makes you feel afraid. Like Ralph, you have to watch out for your OCD bully. You never know when he will show up, or what he will demand of you. You may avoid activities or certain places, even if you would really like to go there, because you are afraid your OCD bully might show up there. Like Ralph, you may try to hide or avoid your OCD bully, or try to get him off your back by doing the things he wants you to do, hoping that he will leave you alone. But he doesn't. He usually will ask more and more things of you—always making more demands.

"The answer to your problem is to learn from Ralph and his situation. Do not try to run or hide from your OCD bully. Do not try to get him to leave you alone by doing what he wants because he will just demand more the next time. Like Ralph, the answer is to stand up to the bully. Show him you are not going to take it anymore. Let him know he can't boss you around the way he used to. Challenge him. Tell him to go jump in a lake! You will find that, like Max, at first he will make some attempts to keep you under his control, but if you keep with it, he will tire and in the end, he will learn that he can no longer control you the way he used to and will tend to leave you alone."

Although the same is true for most of the stories in this book, this story in particular should be referenced repeatedly in treatment, helping the child (or adult) to keep the perspective of an anthropomorphized OCD. A living and dynamic relationship between the OCD client and the OCD itself results in giving structure and purpose to the treatment. It provides an excellent framework from which the client can mobilize and direct his emotional energies.

A living and dynamic relationship between the OCD client and the OCD itself results in giving structure and purpose to the treatment.

7

Trust

Trust is of paramount importance to the success of nearly all types of therapies for all types of psychiatric difficulties. This is nowhere more evident than in the cognitive behavioral therapy of OCD, when the client is relying on the therapist to guide him and support him as he directly faces his deepest, darkest fears. The following set of stories discuss the issue of trust, where trusting what you shouldn't trust, and not trusting what you should, can sometimes cause difficulties.

Dr. Einhorn

It is funny how the tiniest moments in time can stay with a person decades after the moment has passed. When I was eight years old, I had my appendix taken out. About three weeks after my discharge from the hospital, my mother took me to our family physician to have the stitches removed, since this was well before the time surgeons regularly used dissolvable stitches.

I wasn't particularly nervous about going to the doctor because I hadn't really thought much about it, but then I found myself sitting alone with the doctor in his examing room, with him holding a pair of tweezers that were headed for my abdomen. He had said, "Don't worry, it won't hurt," but as he approached me, I pushed his hand away and said I was afraid. He reiterated, "Don't worry, Allen, it really won't hurt at all." As he approached again, I recoiled with what I imagine must have been terror on my face.

My doctor, who had been our family physician since before I was born, slid back his chair, which was on rollers, about a foot or so from me. He took a slow breath, and then, looking directly into my eyes, he said in a slow, calm voice, "Allen, have I ever told you that something wasn't going to hurt when it ended up hurting? Have I ever lied to you about something hurting you?" My mind started to search.

I thought of several times when he had told me in advance that a needle was going to pinch, or that removing a bandage would cause some burning. I even remembered once, when I needed to get what had seemed like a particularly large injection, that he very clearly warned me that it would probably hurt more than a little bit, and that if I wanted to, I could yell out my favorite song while he gave me the shot because he thought it might help. It did hurt, and he was right, the singing (the Beatles' "Do You Want to Know a Secret?") helped. As I searched my mind, I also realized that there were times when he had performed a procedure of one kind or another on me and had told me that it wouldn't hurt, and I could not remember even one instance when it did.

In these same moments, I remembered wondering why I didn't trust what he was saying given his history of being so honest with me. It was then that I realized that my mother, who was from an older school of thought, would often tell me that something would not hurt when in fact it ended up being quite painful. There was the time she had sprayed one of my scrapes, and her promise of no pain was followed by an intense burning sensation. On another occasion, she told me that I would feel only the slightest tug as she pulled out a splinter. It ended up hurting terribly. It was then that I made the cognitive jump to the realization that not *all* grownups misrepresented the truth about the prospect of pain. Under circumstances related to pain, my mom often did not tell the truth, but my doctor always did.

I made the cognitive jump to the realization that not all *grownups misrepresented the truth about the prospect of pain.*

In that moment of realization, in that second of recognition that this was my doctor, and not my mother, and that therefore I could trust him completely when he said it would not hurt as he pulled out my stitches, in that tiny slice of time so many decades ago, I remember clearly the feeling of the fear leaving my body, as if I were a beach ball deflating. In completely turning myself over into his hands, the struggle ended. I remember feeling my muscles loosen up, my breathing becoming more calm and regular, and my heartbeat slowing down.

The OCD Connection

Trust was the prescription I received from my doctor that day. It was trust that allowed me to give up a defensive, protective stance, submitting myself to what lay before me with the calming thought that it would all be OK. This is the challenge that OCD sufferers face in their quest for dominance over their disorder.

When an OCD client is faced with a behavioral exposure exercise, trust plays an important role in determining the intensity and duration of his or her anxiety response. So often clients talk to me about their thoughts and feelings in those moments before facing an exposure experience. "This will be more than I can bear … I will be overwhelmed at a later time because of what I will do here, and then it will be too late or difficult to fix or undo." What they lack is trust. They lack the trust that their own bodies and minds can endure the hardship; trust that they are up to the task; trust that the therapist knows the OCD inside of them even better than they do, at least with regard to how it will respond to treatment.

If the client can learn to trust that "it's just the OCD," what is generally called "labeling the OCD," then he greatly influences the speed of his habituation and desensitization. If he can believe that what he is thinking and the fear that he is feeling are merely symptoms of his disorder, symptoms that will decrease even more quickly than it feels possible, then he will more easily move forward into the exposure experience, with less conflict and reservation. If he can give up the *perceived* control that his defensive stance is somehow protecting him from some imminent danger, then he can relax. If he can give himself completely over to trust, then he can more quickly let go of the fear and move through his recovery in less time and with less emotional pain.

By trusting Dr. Einhorn and letting go of my fear, I was better able to accept without resistance the medical procedure that previously had triggered high anxiety. The story serves as a wonderful illustration of how trusting in oneself, the therapist, and the clinical procedure will allow a client to move through the exposure process more easily, more quickly, and with significantly lower levels of anxiety and psychological discomfort.

White-Water Rafting

It is the night before you are to go on your first white-water rafting trip. You feel excited but terrified. Visions of one of those TV commercials selling something that you cannot recall dwell in your mind's eye.

In the ad there are a group of guys in helmets bouncing up and down in a twelve-man raft while traveling down a raging river in Colorado. At times the raft is completely airborne, and the men, drenched, and seemingly in mortal danger, are surrounded by walls of white, charging water. Your friend who has invited you on this adventure has reassured you that the water on this trip is described as "Class III" rapids, meaning that they were relatively calm, and nothing like those TV commercials, but you don't know the actual people who organized the trip, so how do you know that they really know the truth, or if you can trust their assessment? You are aware of the fact that they need a certain number of guys in order to fill two six-man rafts, and maybe they told your friend anything, just so that you and he would join them, with the expectation that you would somehow manage once out there, holding on for dear life.

And of course, once you *are* out there, what choice would you have? You would be trapped, like a rider on a roller coaster that you did not feel ready to handle; but once you are strapped in, and you find yourself being pulled up that first, long, precarious incline, well, it's just too late to do anything about it, isn't it? You've got to bite the bullet, white-knuckle it, and hold on, right?

Anyway, these are the thoughts that are racing through your head the night before this big trip. You get up nice and early and drive to the drop-off point, north along the river. You pay the entrance fee, and sign away your life, putting your name on a document that essentially says that you or your family will not sue the rafting company if you get injured or killed during your day of fun and relaxation on the water. This in no way helps your impending sense of panic and doom.

But then things get better, and you are somewhat reassured. There are rafting lessons, where the people who work at the rafting site review with you where you will be going, what you will be doing, and how you should work as a group to negotiate the water and rocks. You actually sit in several rafts out of the water that are propped up on logs, taking what is essentially a fifteen-minute class, where you are instructed on how to use your weight and work as a team to negotiate the rapids and get loose if you get stuck on a rock.

You are also reassured by the fact that these rafting employees will be escorting you down the river, themselves in kayaks, which allows them to quickly run in between and around the rafts, should you need any kind of assistance. It also helps that you aren't issued helmets, indicating that they don't think, at least in your mind, that you will be needing them. Finally, you carefully review all the other people who are getting instruction with you, and for every person whom you deem to be under fourteen or over fifty, you are able to breathe a little more easily. Surely if *they* could handle this, so could you!

And so off you go. For the first few minutes, things are very calm. You are moving at a nice pace, but the river is wide, and there are no obstructions of any kind. The surface of the river is completely smooth.

Soon though, you can see the white water up ahead. There are large rocks protruding from the water all over the place, and there is rushing water everywhere. The water is indeed white, and there is no way around it—you are headed straight for it and are going to go right through it. Your heart begins to race, your breathing quickens, and your muscles tighten. You clutch your paddle so that the blood in your body does not feel as though it is reaching your hands. You have visions of being thrown out of the raft, striking your unprotected head against one of those giant boulders, and being submerged by the oncoming rush of water.

Your heart begins to race, your breathing quickens, and your muscles tighten.

As you approach the area of white water, all these feelings and thoughts intensify. It is almost as if you are going in slow motion, and it seems to be taking forever to reach the area that you had spotted from a distance. Your raft mates start to shout out comments: "Hold on!!" and "Here it comes!!" ring through your ears, as does the sound of rushing water, which seems to grow louder with each second.

And then, surprised, you find that it has ended. You are through it and on the other side. The ride had been bumpy and fun, maybe even somewhat exhilarating, but not nearly the death-defying, roller-coaster challenge that you had envisioned. You think to yourself, "Gee, that really wasn't bad at all." Emboldened, you look forward, searching out the next area of rough waters.

This comes soon enough. Around the bend there is a large area of very rough water. You can hear the roar even before turning the corner and visually detecting the white between the patches of gray and blue. From a distance, it looks quite formidable, and as you get closer, the boulders protruding from the center of the river come more clearly into view, intensifying the precariousness of the situation. In a moment you have lost all your brazenness, and once again you are fraught with anticipatory anxiety. Again, the roar increases in your ears, and warnings are shouted out by the other rafters. This time, as with the first set of rapids, you find that as soon as you are in calm waters again, you feel not only relieved but also silly for having been so anxious on the approach.

This happened several more times during the early hours of your trip, but as the day progresses, you learn to react differently to the sight of white water. You learn to trust that what appeared to be dangerous and potentially overwhelming was neither. You learn *not to trust* your own initial fear reaction and instead remind yourself that you are completely capable of handling this level of rapids and that all the previous experiences have proven to you that the end result did not warrant the anticipatory anxiety.

The OCD Connection

The connection to recovery from OCD is obvious. One of the biggest challenges in exposure therapy is learning that anticipatory anxiety is indeed an overreaction to the upcoming situation. Learning not to trust that first flood of thoughts, "I won't be able to handle it—it will be too much for me," is quite a difficult task. But through repeated exposure, much like the repeated encounters with the rapids, a client can learn to reevaluate that experience of anticipatory anxiety and remind herself not to trust those thoughts that betray her, the thoughts that tell her that she will not be able to cope with the consequences of engaging in her exposure and response prevention exercises. Once done, this frees her up for the more frequent, more intense exposures that will ultimately give her the power to resist her rituals and allow her to successfully overcome avoidance.

By telling clients the story of White-Water Rafting, therapists can help clients to better question and doubt their own anticipatory anxiety. This will serve to increase their willingness to move forward in their exposure hierarchies and with less emotional pain and anxiety.

Therapists can help clients to better question and doubt their own anticipatory anxiety.

Driving on Route 27

In Central New Jersey there is a major road that runs through several towns. It is called by a different name depending on the town in which it is located, but throughout and on maps it is referred to as Route 27. Route 27 is a four-lane road with two lanes of traffic in each direction. You can drive reasonably fast on this road, 35 to 45 miles per hour and still be driving within the legal limits. Because there is no divider of any kind between the two inner lanes, with drivers from opposite directions each traveling at about the speed limit, you can be approaching a car that is approaching you at a combined speed of about 90 miles an hour with, maybe, 4 feet of space between the two cars as they pass each other on the road. This set of circumstances makes good fodder for a discussion with someone who suffers from OCD.

The OCD Connection

More than anything else, fighting OCD is about doing things that feel risky. Persons with OCD often acknowledge this, but then they report that they themselves are not good risk takers. They have difficulty moving forward without having a pretty good sense that things are guaranteed to work out all right. They ask, "Well how do you know that I don't really have this disease? I need to check to make sure I am OK"; or, "I can't be sure that I didn't hit somebody. I have to drive back and look again"; or, "How do I know that somebody isn't going to get sick because I didn't clean up properly in the kitchen?"

Typically, the response of the casual observer might be an attempt at a rational discussion, looking at the probabilities, evidence, history, or any other sources of information that might support the idea that the person's worries were overreactive or even completely unfounded. Well, if the worrier in fact has OCD, we know this is a complete waste of time. We know that any attempt at reassurance is bound to fail because, in the obsessive world of OCD, the quest for guarantees is bound to fail. You never really *can* know for sure.

And so the more OCD-educated bystander might take a different strategic position in her response to the person with OCD. She will not attempt to reassure him but, rather, will challenge the person with OCD to accept the idea that he can *never* know for sure whether the thing he is concerned about will actually happen or not. "But how," wonders the person with OCD, "can one exist with such doubt? How can I function without knowing? How do I dare take the risks of not doing that extra check, of not spending another moment on my ritual just to make sure that the dreaded consequence will not happen? It is just not in me to be able to do that!"

And that is where we bring in Route 27. "How did you get here today?" the therapist can ask of the client in therapy. If your office is located in Central New Jersey, very often the answer is, among other roads, "Route 27." And the therapist can explain how, when driving on this road, you essentially come within 6 feet or less of opposing traffic with both traveling at a combined speed that is potentially deadly should you hit another car head on. The therapist can go on to say, "These are strangers driving those approaching vehicles—hundreds of strangers passing within 4 feet of you. Minute after minute they keep approaching and then passing you, but you don't know who they are. You don't know *anything* about these people. They could be depressed and suicidal; they could be drunk. They could be fighting with their ex-spouse about custody issues on the cell phone. They could be distracted playing with the GPS controls or with their iPod. Isn't that true?"

The client is likely to respond, "Yeah, I guess so ..." to which the therapist can then say, "Well then, why do you keep on driving? You could get killed! Why take the risk?"

And usually, after a brief pause, comes the sheepish response, "Well, I don't really think about that, I just do it."

"But what about the risks?" the therapist asks.

The client responds, "But you *have* to take a chance. You have to drive, or else you can't get anywhere, you can't do anything. You have to just kind of trust that it will turn out OK."

"Ahhhh ..." concludes the therapist, "So there it is!"

This leads to a further elaboration of the idea that your client in fact takes risks every moment of every day. "You could, after all, choke to death on your food, fall down the stairs in your home or in your shower and break your neck, suffer a heart attack or a stroke without having any warning or medical history that would make you a likely candidate as a cardiac risk," and on and on. And in fact each of these things *do* happen. People really *do* die of car accidents on state highways. People *do* die from freak home accidents or choking on their food or from unexpected illnesses. This kind of unexpected occurrence happens *every day.* On the other hand, where is it documented that anybody ever got AIDS by seeing a

Your client in fact takes risks every moment of every day.

thin "gay looking" man from across the parking lot? Or that if a person thinks of his parent dying while he walks through a doorway and then doesn't go back and repeat the walk through the threshold thinking something positive that the parent will indeed die? Or that someone accidentally killed her whole family by unknowingly putting poison in with the cookie batter?

The important thing to keep in mind here is that as the therapist you are *not* trying to convince clients that their fears are less likely to come true than any of these other events. You are *not* saying, "You are less likely to have this feared consequence happen if you put off your compulsion than these other things that happen in real life every day," because that would be looking at probabilities of the risks, something, that, as mentioned earlier, goes nowhere in an OCD-related conversation. The point that you as therapist *are* trying to make with clients is that these concerns, these feared consequences that they struggle with, have *nothing* to do with risks at all. They are about having OCD. Pure and simple. They are arbitrary. They are just random ideas that become mediums for the expression of OCD.

By pointing out that the person *does* take risks on a daily basis without thinking about it, such as driving on Route 27, risks that in fact *do* on occasion have negative consequences, we hope to demonstrate to clients that having difficulty confronting OCD is not about being a person who has difficulty taking risks, or difficulty trusting. The client does in fact take risks, and often. And he does this by trusting that things will be OK, even without knowing for sure.

People with OCD already trust, in a thousand ways every day and without guarantees that things will turn out all right. They need to recognize and accept this and transfer this cognitive and behavioral repertoire to their OCD struggle. This translates into recognizing that the struggle is not about risk taking but about having OCD, and that they can trust without being sure, just as they do all the time in so many other situations.

8

Lapses and Relapses

By its very nature, OCD waxes and wanes. Even when treatment is successful, clients are at risk for lapses in their recovery, or even on occasion a complete relapse, with a return to a previous level of functioning. The following stories are designed to be used by therapists in helping their clients keep their perspective about these "bumps in the road," and learn to better anticipate and negotiate these fluctuations in levels of OCD symptoms and the resulting variability in healthy functioning.

Fishing

Steve is nine years old, and he loves to fish. Nothing fancy, mind you, just your standard "worm on a hook and red and white bobber" kind of fishing. He would cast his line out, let it settle in the water, reel in the slack, and sit with an intense gaze on that bobber, wishing for it to vibrate and create concentric circles in the water.

When the fish that took the bait was a small one, it was all fairly straightforward—set the hook by giving a good tug on the line and then reel 'er in as fast as he could, thinking that if he waited too long his catch might somehow break free. With sunnies and other smaller fish, this technique worked every time. But this strategy would often fail Steve when the fish was a larger one. With larger fish, the line would go out further before Steve even had the chance to pick up his fishing pole, requiring him to reel in more line before bringing the fish home. The fish, being larger, would better match his strength, and, as he tried to use his standard strategy of reeling the fish in as quickly as possible, the fish would often interrupt this process and stop Steve dead in his tracks. In those seconds, the fish would be pulling in one direction, and

Steve would be pulling with all his might in the other, and the line would not move at all.

Sometimes Steve would prevail, the fish would tire, and he would once again continue his relentless efforts to reel the fish in, ultimately making the catch. Sometimes, however, the fish held out, and the stalemate continued until, all of a sudden, the line went limp. Thinking naively that he must have tired the fish out, he would then once again furiously reel the line in to an ultimate disappointment—the fish had gotten away.

On one occasion when this particular drama played itself out, Steve was in a canoe with a friend and his older cousin, who witnessed the entire scene. The older cousin sat Steve down and taught him that when the fish was a bigger one, an alternative strategy was required.

Essentially, the art of catching the big fish is to "play" with it. You reel it in until you hit that "stalemate" point, the point when the fish is pulling away with all its strength. At that moment, you let up, allowing the fish to pull away a bit, using up more of its strength. When it begins to tire and the pull on your line lightens up a bit, you once again reel in with all of your might.

The bottom line is, you don't try to land the fish completely in one try. You let it "win" a little bit every now and then, allowing it to swim a little further out for a while, with the understanding that, in the big picture you are tiring him out, so that that when all is said and done, you catch him.

The OCD Connection

When it comes to OCD, the "big fish" strategy tends to be the strategy of choice. Often, when OCD clients are in treatment, they are very enthusiastic about doing battle with their OCD. They want to eradicate it completely and want to eliminate it immediately from every aspect of their lives. Although having strong motivation and feeling powerful is certainly a plus, this kind of very black-and-white thinking has its drawbacks.

These clients want to "reel in" the OCD at every opportunity, right from the start, without ever giving in to it. In essence, they are using the "small fish" strategy. The problem is, invariably the OCD does win out on occasion, and the person gives in to the compulsion to check or wash, or whatever behavior the OCD demands. In these cases the OC client will often become devastated, feel guilty, depressed, and weak, devalue the behavioral treatment intervention, and may even give up trying, letting the OCD continue to dominate. To continue with our analogy, the big fish gets away when you use a "small fish" strategy.

It is preferable to recognize that you need to "play" with the OCD, choose your battles, letting the OCD have its way every now and then. As long as you pace yourself and fight the OCD on your own terms, you will ultimately win out and reel in that big fish.

You may also find that as you beat down the OCD for a particular symptom, it may reemerge with a different symptom or come back as the same symptom at a later time. This, too, can be disheartening to the person with OCD. What is helpful to remember here is that each time you beat down the OCD you make *it* weaker, and you strengthen *your* own battle skills against it. Because of this, beating it down for a second or third time, or beating down the second or third kind of symptom, may go more quickly and require less effort.

Although this is not always the case, it often is. Each time the OCD comes back, whether in its original form or as a new symptom, it is like the big fish pulling out a little extra line. Don't get alarmed. Patiently reel it in again, tiring it out a little more each time. Ultimately, you have a better chance of landing the big fish.

Clients in therapy will often exhibit black-and-white thinking, and will interpret a single experience where they cave in to the demands of OCD as a major failure, and perhaps even as an indication that they are not up to the task of doing ERP work. This of course can have disastrous effects on motivation to continue with the ERP form of treatment. Therapists can utilize the Fishing Story under such circumstances as a way to help reframe such a "failure" as merely part of the process of "landing the big fish." By essentially giving the client permission to give in to his OCD urges on occasion, you decrease the intensity of pressure to perform perfectly, and you set up a situation where on those occasions when the client is not able to resist compulsive urges, he is less likely to experience a sense of defeat and perhaps even of depression.

By essentially giving the client permission to give in to his OCD urges on occasion, you decrease the intensity of pressure to perform perfectly.

Financial Advice

Mitch is a financial advisor. He has many clients who trust in his advice and invest their life savings according to his suggestions. One of Mitch's clients is Fred. Like millions of other people throughout the world, Mitch had a terrible year financially in 2008. His retirement vehicles are worth half of what they were just two years ago. Fred feels as though he would have done better financially had he put his money slated for retirement under his pillow. Fred would meet quarterly with Mitch to discuss his finances, and each time they met Fred complained to him, telling him that he felt that he was going backward and that, the more money he seemed to put into his accounts, the more he lost. It made him want to stop trying altogether.

At these meetings, Mitch would look at him and heave a heavy sigh. He would acknowledge that Fred had in fact lost money that he had put into his retirement account over the last couple of years but stress that Fred had to take a larger perspective. He would explain that Fred was only in his late thirties and would have plenty of time to recover from the present market trend. Mitch would take out a graph and show Fred that the stock market tends to wax and wane over time, sometimes up, sometimes down, and that, although many people claimed to understand these fluctuations, there was really no way to know for sure what was going to happen next and why things happened the way they did.

He did say, however, that the one thing that you could pretty much count on was that the market, *in the long run*, was steadily heading up. He showed Fred that for any twenty-year period of time, beginning at any time over the last hundred years, even during the years of the Great Depression in the 1930s and the major drop in the market in 1987, the market was still rising at a rate of approximately 7 percent annually. He demonstrated that if you look at a graph of the market's performance over the last two years, you would see a line going sharply down, making it look like investing money in the market was a poor choice. But if you looked at a larger period of time, and stretched the graph back another eighteen years, you could clearly see that the last few years was a dip in a line that overall had been climbing steadily.

"Think in the long term. Keep a larger perspective. See the recent losses as just a 'blip' in an otherwise upwards trend." These are the words that Fred repeated to himself like a mantra as he put the effort into writing yet another monthly check to be deposited into the declining account. These are the words he held onto when he looked at his statements each month with their disappointing figures. "Don't lose track of your goal. Keep your eyes on the prize. Trust in the process."

The OCD Connection

And so it is with OCD. So many clients will say, after having made a certain amount of progress, "I seem not to be going anywhere," or, "I'm going backward." They complain that they don't see the dividends of their efforts and that their hard work does not seem to be paying off. They say that they feel that the medication and/or the ERP are not working for them as well anymore, that they are tired, that they want to give up and give into the OCD, rather than fighting all the time. They get depressed.

This is not unusual. And although sometimes the medication does indeed need to be "tweaked," or the ERP needs to be redesigned somewhat, or, in fact, a break from treatment may be warranted, most of the time the person with OCD needs only what Fred needed from Mitch: a little encouragement, a little faith in the process, and a redirection toward the larger perspective. Clients need to understand that a spike in symptoms do not necessarily indicate that they are going backward, but rather it is just a "blip" in the otherwise upward trend in their recovery process.

It is important for therapists to help clients remember where they were when they first started treatment and to help them acknowledge for themselves how far they have come. And although it is true that some people are more treatment resistant than others, you can share with your clients that there is no reason to believe that they in particular cannot be helped by those interventions that we know to be helpful for most people with OCD. You can point out that this is true especially when these interventions have helped this client in the past.

Sometimes the client asks, "Why am I not doing as well now as I have done previously? Why do I seem to be losing ground?" This is not always easy to understand. We could point to changes in the client's life situation or stressors that have been introduced in his recent past, but it still comes down to the fact that in general, OCD is a disorder that waxes and wanes, and so by definition, the course of recovery is often interrupted by periods of decline.

It seems that the most important things at times like these are support and encouragement—in communicating hope and faith in your client's abilities to weather the tougher times so that ultimately he will prevail. Like the wise choices in the financial markets, medication and behavioral treatment of OCD still provide a winning investment in the long term.

More Financial Advice from Mitch

Fred, whom we first met in the story Financial Advice, was having one of his quarterly meetings with Mitch, and things were looking pretty good. His portfolio of retirement investments was increasing, but he was still complaining. He looked at his totals, looked at his age, and felt that he would never reach his financial goals. He felt way behind where he thought he should be. It seemed like such a long, long way off, to make up for all those years when he was not in the position to invest money for his retirement.

As previously, Mitch sighed and smiled. "You're looking at this the wrong way, Fred," he said. "You have to look at where you are now compared to where you were just recently. This is a better indication of where you are going in the future than your general sense of where you 'should be.'"

"You have to look at where you are now compared to where you were just recently. This is a better indication of where you are going in the future than your general sense of where you 'should be.'"

Mitch explained that although Fred did need to be vigilant in continuing to put away money for retirement, and that although there was, indeed, a lot of catching up to do, it was important for him to pay close attention to the fact that, in just a short period of time, he had significantly increased his entire retirement investment. Fred was beating himself up for not doing things years ago that he really could not have done anyway, and he was ignoring the important improvements in his investment portfolio that he had instituted more recently. He was looking in the wrong place, feeling bad about choices made a long time ago, rather than feeling satisfied and proud about what he was able to do more recently.

The OCD Connection

Here, too, we find that Mitch has a message for people struggling with OCD. Often clients come to therapy with a long list of OCD symptoms. Their lives are disrupted in so many ways. The OCD manifests itself throughout the day in a variety of mental or behavioral disruptions. It is very hard to know where to start.

Through the course of treatment, we define our starting point and stay focused, narrowing down our interventions to target only those symptom manifestations that are contracted to focus on. Usually progress is made relatively quickly, especially when the client is determined and works hard to face fears and put the time in that is required for proper ERP. Invariably, however, the person with OCD, the parent, or the significant other will bemoan the fact that "there is so much work left to do."

It is not unlike the obese person who is reluctant to congratulate him- or herself for losing those first 10 pounds, or the smoker who is reticent to even tell people that it has been a week since his last cigarette. It is easy to get caught up into looking at the mountain of challenges yet to come and to completely disregard having successfully negotiated the biggest challenge of all: getting started!

When Mitch asked Fred to focus on his recent accomplishments and to see the strength that lies in that, it made him feel more empowered and helped him to believe that, somehow, he will be able to reach the goals that he had set for himself. In starting to put the money aside, he had already put into place a mindset and a behavioral style of money management that had not existed previously. This is what would make it possible for him to realize his goals in ways that were impossible before. To think that he should have started earlier only works against this sense of empowerment and, ultimately, against achieving these goals.

With the OCD-afflicted person, as with the cigarette smoker who is quitting or the obese person who has begun to lose weight, focusing on what has already been achieved, and seeing this accomplishment as an indication of what might be, are essential to the maintenance of further progress. Any sports coach (or sports psychologist, for that matter) will tell you that a person's mindset is *at least* as important to his ultimate success as an athlete as is his or her physical ability and time spent practicing. Performance relies on a positive sense of empowerment and self-efficacy (the belief that one does something well, that one is capable).

Therefore, it is important for the person actively involved in treatment for OCD to find that delicate balance between looking at what yet needs to be accomplished, setting goals, and thinking in terms of one's overall direction on the one hand, while on the other hand recognizing and celebrating personal progress to date, and allowing one's self to be proud of whatever movement has been made so far, however small. Bringing forth the story More Financial Advice from Mitch serves the purpose of illustrating in a very concrete way (and what might be a very relevant way depending on the status of the financial markets) these basic ideas. The result is again an increase in positive feelings for the client regarding his or her present level of functioning, leading to an increase in motivation to continue to work on the problem.

Growing Like Weeds

Many families have grandparents living in another part of the country and make it a tradition of visiting them once a year over certain holidays when schools are closed or over winter break or summer vacation. Invariably, during these visits, the family will meet up with the grandparents' friends and neighbors, some of whom have not seen the out-of-towners since the last visit. The comments about the children tend to be positive and complimentary and run something like this, "Ooh! What good-looking children! So cute!" etc. However, some version of, "My, they are growing like weeds!" indicating that the children have substantially grown over the intervening year is almost always part of the series of the remarks spoken.

The parents in this family, who may not be as keenly aware at any given moment of the growth spurts of their children, will easily concede, once these comments are spoken, that their children do grow like weeds! This observation is intensified when parents view the older photos of their children that are usually displayed all around the grandparents' home. It is an interesting phenomenon that, living with them day to day, it is hard for parents to be aware of the amazingly rapid changes that take place in their children's physical development over the course of time. It is only through the eyes of those who see them but once a year that the miracle of their growth is clearly apparent.

It seems that this dynamic exists for just about anything that changes slowly over time. It is hard to notice small changes on a regular basis, and the impact of gradual change is only easily recognized if occasional inspection of some kind is done so that one can compare the progress of change over a certain interval of elapsed time.

It is hard to notice small changes on a regular basis.

The OCD Connection

This is the case as well with progress made in any program of recovery. With OCD, although changes can often be dramatic and swift, sometimes the struggle for freedom from domination by rituals and obsessions is slow and agonizing. Especially on particularly "bad OCD days," or even during bad OCD weeks, it is sometimes hard for clients to feel as though it is worth keeping up the fight. It is for this reason that written record-keeping exercises are such an integral part of a successful recovery program for OCD.

By keeping written records of subjective units of discomfort, or SUDs, a scale of 0–100 (or sometimes 0–10) measuring the intensity of one's emotional discomfort and anxiety, we can measure people's progress to their exposure experiences when employing ERP over a period of time. In this way one is able to more clearly see the progress that is invariably made over the course of many weeks or months. In an exposure experience where a SUDs level has for some reason increased to 55 for something that was only a 45 two days ago, it is easy to forget that the same exposure experience had been a whopping 85 when first attempted two weeks earlier. Under conditions of slow change, it is only through this larger perspective achieved by reviewing long-term records that one can fully appreciate the fruits of one's efforts.

Therefore, it is highly recommended that you advise your clients to actually keep a written record of their SUDs levels at the start and end of each exposure experience and, under some conditions, even make a note of the levels at regular intervals during the course of a single exposure session. In this way clients can better recognize and report to you the progress that has been attained. This reinforces the faith that the technique works (which itself aids in the application of ERP for the next challenge) and helps one to maintain an overall positive and hopeful attitude toward overcoming OCD through the application of ERP techniques. Growing Like Weeds is one of those stories that most people can relate to on a personal level, and so it helps clients to understand the difficulties that sometimes exist in recognizing change. This sets them up to be more receptive to the task of written record keeping and reporting.

9

Special Topics

This chapter contains a potpourri of stories that address different issues that commonly come up when one is treating OCD. These include resistance to discussing the details of symptoms, the OCD presentations of hoarding and health anxiety, OCD compulsions that are done without specific limits but until the client feels "just right," and family involvement in rituals.

Talking to the Alien

You're a father, and your family is getting dressed to go to an affair. Your twelve-year-old son approaches you and asks you to teach him how to tie his necktie. He had gone shopping with your wife the week before, and they had decided together that he was now old enough to buy a real tie, graduating up from the fake clip-on ones.

As you stand next to him in front of the large bathroom mirror, each of you with an unmade tie around your respective necks, you realize that you have no clue as how to explain to him how to make the knot. You find this curious, as you have put on a tie for work every workday for years and have never given it a second thought. But now, standing in front of the mirror with your son, you realize, that you never really *think* about it. You just *do* it.

Resolved to fulfill your fatherly obligations, you take a deep breath and position your hands on the two ends of your tie. Surprised, you find that, repeatedly, you are unable to explain to your son the complete series of moves needed to successfully make the knot. You try by instructing your son on a couple of the initial hand movements required to get started, and then you find that suddenly you are at a loss as to how to proceed. You undo the tie to restart the process from the beginning, and again get stuck at a certain point, amazed that you are struggling so with an activity that has so long been part of your daily routine. You untie the tie and begin again. This time, without talking to your son at all, without describing verbally what it is that you are doing, you tie the knot, while with a sort of "third eye," you observe the process. It is only then that you are able to go back and explain to him the steps involved in tying the tie. It is as if you had to let the behavior of tying the tie "teach" you what you were aware of only at some unconscious level.

It is interesting how many times and in how many ways this kind of phenomenon can reveal itself over the course of a person's day-to-day life. Perhaps you have experienced it when you tried to teach your daughter how to tie her shoes or swing a baseball bat, when you instructed a teenage neighbor how to drive a car that had a stick shift, or gave an out-of-towner directions to your home. You have to step "outside" of the task and observe yourself doing it in order to know what it is that you are actually doing so that you can explain it to someone else.

A variation of this dynamic occurs as well with regard to ideas, lifestyles, or concepts. For instance, your young child might ask such questions as, "Why do people smoke cigarettes?" or "Why do people say, 'God bless you' when a person sneezes?" and on and on, as small children are apt to do. What this does, as it did when you were teaching your son about the necktie, is to require one to step "outside" of the situation, a situation that we just accept as part of the world we live in. We then have to ask ourselves the question we are being asked and then attempt to explain in basic terms the things that we generally do not even think about.

Of course, when giving the pat answers to some of the more thoughtful and probing questions like, "Why is there prejudice?" or, "Why are there homeless people?" or, "Why are there wars?" we often find that the answers themselves ring hollow, not only for the child, but in our own ears. Many adults report that it was having such discussions with their small children that prompted them to greater involvement in environmental, charitable, or political causes. They report that it helped them to be more aware of the hypocrisy of not acting in response to these situations.

You may recall a movie from the 1970s called, "Star Man," starring Jeff Bridges and Karen Allen. Bridges played an alien, and Allen functioned as a sort of earthling ambassador, explaining to him about how we live and why we do the things that we do. In one scene, they are at a diner, and she orders food for him. When the food arrives, he begins to devour the apple pie before eating his main meal. Allen's character explains, "No, that's dessert—you eat that after."

He asks, "Why?" and, after a few flustered attempts to explain, she just quips at him, "It's just the way we do things!"

Children are kind of like aliens visiting this planet for the first time. The questions that they ask often force us to stop and think of the specifics of what we do and why we do it. It requires us to objectify ourselves regarding our behavior, becoming somewhat separate from that behavior and observing it from a distance.

The OCD Connection

When someone with OCD is experiencing an obsession and is struggling with the idea of executing a compulsion, it is often helpful to speak out loud about it to someone else. It is the explaining of it, especially when the obsession is complicated, "magical," or absurd in some way, that allows the person with OCD to distance him- or herself from the experience, to become more objective.

Often, when clients explain certain symptoms in session for the first time, they will preface by saying, "I know this sounds ridiculous," or "You're going to think I'm crazy." They may even laugh at themselves when telling the specifics of their obsessions. These are all expressions of their ability to objectify themselves, to separate themselves from their symptoms. When reviewing the specifics of their rituals, clients will sometimes forget the exact order, or "what comes next" in the progression of ritualistic behaviors, just as when the father forgot the next step in tying the necktie in the story above. At other times, clients may remember the specifics of even complicated rituals, but cannot remember why they started to do them, or what purpose these continue to serve.

In the treatment of OCD, the ability to objectify oneself, to "stand outside" of one's symptoms, is an important prerequisite to effectively administrating ERP interventions.

In the treatment of OCD, the ability to objectify oneself, to "stand outside" of one's symptoms, is an important prerequisite to effectively administrating ERP interventions. Talking about the specifics of the obsessions experienced and the compulsions being contemplated, then, becomes an important way to distance oneself enough from the experienced OCD symptoms so that ERP interventions can be applied. Like talking to the alien, explaining it out loud to another person provides the prospective necessary to see OCD symptoms *as* symptoms, and to ground oneself in reality in a powerful way. When in the early stages of treatment a client is resistant to discuss details of her symptoms, the therapist can use Talking to the Alien as way of explaining how this sharing helps, not only in the collection of data that will be used to construct the behavioral treatment, but also as a component of treatment itself, helping the client to objectively observe her symptoms, and positioning her to better accept and utilize the ERP treatment to follow.

Aunt Molly's Cookies

Most everybody has one of those older relatives who tries to push food on them during family gatherings. Let us collapse all of these people into a mythical person whom we shall call "Aunt Molly." Aunt Molly was born and raised in Eastern Europe in the early 1900s. She is a wonderful cook, but more than anything else, she loves to bake. Her favorite, and everyone else's, are her apple cookies.

As a child, whenever you would visit her house, she would prepare an elaborate meal, and, completely stuffed, you and the rest of your family would sit around at the dinner table after eating, hardly able to breathe. Aunt Molly would then come out, after already having served at least one or two significant deserts as part of the main meal, carrying a big tray of her famous cookies. Her favorite line was, "Just try one! One couldn't hurt now, could it?" And of course, she was right, one couldn't hurt, and so you usually indulged. However, if you grabbed that first cookie too quickly and she noticed, you can be sure that as you were finishing it, she would again say, "Have another! One more couldn't hurt now, could it?"

No matter how many cookies you had, if you had not pleaded with her, "No more! I can't take another bite!" on the previous cookie, you could bet that upon your finishing that cookie, she would hand you her "couldn't hurt" line again, prodding you to take yet an additional one. The survival strategy of course was to make her work to get you to eat that first cookie, and then perhaps she would not push so hard to get you to eat another one.

The interesting thing about Aunt Molly and her "couldn't hurt" line was that she was absolutely right. Whether you protest that you are too full, or that you are trying to watch your weight, or cut down on sugar, one cookie really *does not* make that much of a difference. And if that is true, well then, the same argument would hold for yet another cookie because it, too, would not make a difference in and of itself. And for every individual cookie that you were presented, the argument continues to stand strong—this one cookie would not make much of a difference in the big scheme of things regarding your sugar or caloric intake or how full you were feeling.

Yes, Aunt Molly was right when you looked at her argument one cookie at a time. But when you looked at the series of cookies that she was trying to get you to ingest, well, the argument just did not hold up as well. Four or five cookies *do* make a difference, even if each one individually really does not. And a dozen cookies, well, it becomes even clearer there that they make a difference. Therefore, those having a problem watching their weight, or who are already very full, or who need to watch their sugar intake need to pay attention to the big picture and guard against looking at just the next mouthful. This is because the next mouthful is not just the next mouthful. It is the next mouthful in a series of mouthfuls, and there comes a time in that series when you have definitely overeaten.

The OCD Connection

The obsessive-compulsive hoarder thinks like Aunt Molly. Let us look at a particularly impaired hoarder, whom we shall call Sally. Sally's house is full of stuff—all kinds of stuff—from the floor to almost the ceiling. All of her house is like this. The plumbing broke several years ago, and she dare not let a plumber in the house lest he see the mess, and so she has not had running water for quite some time. She has no heat in her house. She belongs to an athletic club and takes her showers there. She stays at a relative's when it just gets too cold. And because she has not been able to climb into her kitchen for the last several years, she eats out all the time. Sally's husband had left her long ago because of this problem, and she is also estranged from her adult daughter. Sally has a big problem, and she knows it.

Treatment of such a person typically begins by focusing on one particular area of the house. With Sally, the therapist began by focusing on her garage. When you opened up the garage door, you were faced with a wall of junk. Sally was not ready to have large amounts of the rubbish removed at once, and so the therapist began by sifting through the stuff one item at a time. Sally's remarks were very typical of someone with her problem.

"This book," she might remark to her therapist, "is from the same series of books that I used to read as a child—it has great memories for me—I can't part with it." And so it was decided that she would keep that one. One item could not hurt, anyway. "This, now this is an old toy—sure, it's broken, but I am certain that some poor child somewhere would appreciate it." We can be sure that some poor child somewhere would appreciate this toy, so you cannot really directly argue with that comment. Besides, it is just one item—what is the harm in her keeping just that one thing? "Oh, and this, this is a statue—isn't it beautiful? How can I throw away a perfectly good statue?" And so the therapist agrees to stick that item as well in the "keep" pile.

Now, you can do this all day and everything would end up in the "keep" pile. The error is that you cannott have a rational debate about any one item, because the OCD will always win. Why? Because for nearly every thing that is not completely rotten or rusted, ripped to shreds, or completely soiled (and sometimes even for *those* things), the OCD can make an almost logical and rational argument as to why it makes sense to keep it. It is just like Aunt Molly's cookies. "One more couldn't hurt."

The trick is to not argue one item at a time. The response to Sally's comments needs to be something along the lines of, "You know, you're right—when we look at this thing alone, it *does* make sense to keep it—you never know that it can't be used in the way you say." And then turn her toward the garage so that she can see the big pile, and say, "But every one of those items has a story, a reason for not being thrown out. This is not about the value of these items. This is about having OCD and fighting back. Do you or don't you want this garage cleaned out? Do you or don't you want to have your life back?"

In this way, you keep the focus away from the individual items and keep it on the big picture—the dozen cookies, not one cookie at a time. The story of Aunt Molly's Cookies can be used as a vehicle to demonstrate how hoarders need to look at their collection of hoarded items. When you see each piece as just a part of the whole, it makes it just a bit easier to say—"I can't keep this." Is it possible that someone else could make use of it or that someday you may find a use for it?

Keep the focus away from the individual items and keep it on the big picture—the dozen cookies, not one cookie at a time.

Absolutely! Do not argue with the OCD. Label it, challenge it, and keep your focus on the big picture.

It is important to remember again that the stories in this book do not "tell the whole story" when in comes to the treatment of OCD. Aunt Molly's Cookies is another illustration of that. The problem of hoarding is complex and multifaceted. Stepping back and helping clients to see the whole picture is only a small part of treatment protocol for the complex and challenging problem of hoarding. More than that, organizing and throwing out collected items are themselves only part of the treatment. For example, interrupting and curtailing the purchasing of new items to be hoarded is an essential part of an effective treatment protocol for this problem, but this part of the treatment protocol has not been addressed by this particular story.

Selling Cigarettes

If you are old enough to have watched television in the 1970s, you may recall that at the time cigarette commercials were still allowed to be aired, and TV shows were regularly interrupted with many of these ads. You might also remember a particular commercial for the Salem brand of cigarettes. As was the case with most TV cigarette commercials of the time, the visuals were punctuated with beautiful outdoor scenes wherein sexy, young, attractive, and very healthy-looking men and women were seen engaged in wholesome, healthy activities like walking, biking, and hiking, all the while smoking their cigarettes.

In this particular series of commercials for Salem, there was a running jingle that repeated itself over and over again throughout the commercial spot. It went, "You can take Salem out of the country, but, you can't take the 'country' out of, Sa-lem." In the last few seconds of the commercial, that jingle repeated itself one more time, but it didn't run to completion. Instead, you heard, "You can take Salem out of the country but—" the singing and the music stopped there, the screen went white, and all you heard was the singular sound of a triangle chime being struck.

The advertisers were ingenious. They knew that by repeating the jingle it would become "stuck" in our heads, but even better, if they left out the last few words of the jingle at the end of the spot, we would detect the void, and, in our own minds, complete the jingle, by singing to ourselves "... you can't take the 'country' out of Sa-lem." In so doing we had become more involved in the commercial; in fact, we had become a *part* of it! And as any advertiser knows, there is no better way to impact a consumer than to have him or her become a part of the commercial. (Remember those Yellow Pages ads where you had to figure out what you were looking at before they gave you the answer at the very end of the spot?)

That is why, if today you approach anyone over a certain age and say the first part of the Salem jingle, that person will immediately know, and probably say right out loud, the remainder of it, even though TV spots for cigarettes have been banned for decades.

The Salem advertisers took advantage of a universal psychological principle known as the *Zeigarnik effect*, named after the researcher who discovered it. Essentially, it states that *if* something familiar is presented to us, but it is missing a piece, we will make an attempt to complete it. If you see a line, for instance, that is curved almost all the way around so that its beginning approaches its end point but does not quite touch it, your mind will attempt to "close" the line to form a circle. In fact, you would most probably describe the line as an open circle or an incomplete circle as opposed to a curved line, even though, by definition, this figure is *not* a circle, since it does not go completely around.

The OCD Connection

People with OCD experience the Zeigarnik effect as well, but they take it to a whole new level. This effect plays a very important part in the obsessions and resulting compulsions in OCD. Although this is true for most manifestations of the disorder, including those of washing, cleaning, and checking, it is most evident in the problem of ordering and arranging, as well as repetitive and even tic-like behaviors. People with OCD have an extremely difficult time tolerating things, activities, or situations that are experienced as "incomplete" in some way. It is the need to "tie things up into a nice package with a bow" that drives the compulsive behaviors characteristic of people with OCD. Until things are experienced as "finished," where they can then move on, they are plagued with a kind of distress not unlike what we all experience when we have an itch to scratch.

People with OCD have an extremely difficult time tolerating things, activities, or situations that are experienced as "incomplete" in some way.

Like washers who might say that they need to wash until they feel uncontaminated, or checkers who might say they need to check until they feel assured that the door is locked or that they did not leave anything behind, these people say that they need to arrange or order objects, or repeat their body movements until it "just feels right." Unlike checkers and washers, there is no explanation as to why the behavior needs to be repeated or continued. It is not about feeling safe or clean or averting a future danger. It is just about scratching that itch. This phenomenon has been called "Tourettic OCD," a term coined by Dr. Charlie Mansuetto.

That very slight tension that we feel when the TV commercial jingle ends midsentence, or when the line does not quite make it all around to form a circle, begging us to attempt to complete it so that we can feel a certain sense of satisfaction and can then move on, is very much like Touretic OCD. Here, once again, OCD has taken a relatively common and benign human tendency and exaggerated it to such a point that it interferes with the capacity for proper daily functioning, characteristic of a psychiatric symptom. This indeed may add to the difficulty that clients sometimes experience when they complain that they are not sure whether their compulsive drive is within normal limits or truly an OCD symptom. The answer, of course, lies with the degree of distress they experience, the degree to which they can control their behavior, and finally, the degree to which the symptoms interfere with functioning.

Family members in particular will often find it difficult to understand the concept that their OCD-afflicted relative needs to engage in a particular ritual until it "just feels right." Explaining concepts like the Zeigarnic effect, and using examples such as cigarette commercials or unfinished circles helps to communicate about this OCD dynamic.

Mushroom Pizza

When I was a kid, I spent many summers in the Catskill Mountains in upstate New York. My family would live in what was called a "bungalow colony," which was a small collection of cottages surrounded by fields and trees. This community of a couple of dozen closely knit families with young children participated in many activities together. There was a community swimming pool and the "casino," a large cottage where we played bingo on Thursday nights, watched projection movies on Friday nights, and where the adults had some form of entertainment (such as a second-rate comedian or a lesser known singer) on Saturdays. There was a day camp on the grounds and even a small grocery store.

There were no TVs or telephones in the cottages, but there was a single phone in the grocery store. A phone call for anyone at the colony was received there, broadcast by the grocery clerk over the public address (PA) system, a loudspeaker that anyone, anywhere on the bungalow colony grounds could hear, and the recipient of the call would then have to run from wherever she was and go to the grocery store to pick up the phone call.

All of the mothers were stay-at-home moms, and most families owned only one car. Fathers would leave on Sunday night and go home to New York City, work at their jobs through the week, and then return late Friday afternoon. This meant that during the week there were not very many dads around, and very few cars in our parking lot.

Because there were no roads inside the colony itself, and because we were a private community where everyone knew each other, the entire bungalow colony served as a playground for me and all my friends. Growing up in an apartment in Queens, I cherished this kind of freedom to come and go as I pleased.

These memories of carefree summers were briefly shattered one year when I was about ten. I walked into the cottage late one afternoon and saw my mother bending over my sister, who was about fourteen at the time. My sister's face was all puffed up and her eyes were swollen shut. She was grabbing at her throat gasping for air, yelling that she couldn't breathe in a voice that sounded as if she were talking under water. As I walked through the door, my mother shouted at me to go get our neighbor, one of the few people in our community who had a car on the premises during the week. I was to tell our neighbor that we had an emergency and needed her to drive us to the doctor immediately. But I was in shock at the sight of my sister, and stood, transfixed, staring at what looked like—some kind of an alien creature. After what seemed like several minutes but was probably only a few seconds, my mother shouted out to me again, "Go now!"

This I did, and in minutes my mother and sister were gone in the car, and I stood alone on the porch of our cottage trembling from the experience. I had no idea if I would see my sister alive again. About two hours later, they returned, and my sister was fine. It was explained that my sister had had an allergic reaction to mushrooms on pizza that she had eaten earlier in the day, a food allergy that we previously had not been aware of. An epinephrine injection from the physician reversed her condition immediately and completely. As of this writing, my sister has yet to try eating another mushroom.

Fast forward fifteen years from the days at the bungalow colony. I am now in graduate school, it is late spring, and I have been struggling with allergy symptoms since the trees started to bloom. It was now the end of the semester; I needed to be studying for finals, and therefore I could not take any of the medications that had previously helped me because they all had the side effect of severe drowsiness. I was miserable.

Each night, in the middle of a deep sleep, at about 3 a.m., I would awaken and feel that my tongue and the inside of my mouth and throat had become slightly swollen. This would send me into a panic, and I would worry that I was going to choke to death on my own tongue or by my throat closing up and blocking my airway. I would wake up, check my tongue in the mirror repeatedly, drink cold water, and chew on ice cubes as a way of trying to calm myself and reduce the symptoms. Because I did not dare go back to sleep, to try to distract myself and calm down, I would watch television. This went on night after night, and I started to become quite frustrated and anxious, worried that I would not be able to study properly for my finals because I was not getting enough sleep.

During one of these night episodes, I felt particularly angry about my situation—I was exhausted and just wanted to go to bed. And that is when I noticed a very interesting thing about my condition. While I was up in the middle of the night watching television, I would tend to watch old black-and-white movies on a station with lots of commercials. I noticed that while the movie was on and I was absorbed in watching it, I barely noticed any physical discomfort and felt virtually no anxiety. However, as soon as the commercials came on, I would start to focus on my throat, my tongue, and my breathing and get panicky again. When the movie returned to the screen, I once again forgot about my difficulties and just watched the film. I realized more fully at that moment that, while I was experiencing a true physical reaction to seasonal allergens, my anxiety to this condition was indeed an overreaction. I was projecting danger when there really was none, and I was having some kind of associative reaction based on that day, so many years ago, in the bungalow colony when I had watched my sister desperately gasping for air. But I was tired. This just had to stop. I needed to take action.

"This is it!" I said to myself. "I have had it!"

I got up, walked out of the living room, and stood in the middle of the kitchen. I spread my arms outward to my sides, and closed my eyes. "If I am going to choke to death, let it happen, let it be over!" I imagined in my mind's eye that my throat was completely closing up, that I was about to pass out, fall to the floor, and die right there and then. I further pictured that a neighbor would eventually phone the police because of the stench from my apartment, and they would find my decaying body weeks later.

To my surprise, almost immediately, my anxiety about asphyxiating plummeted. Although I could still feel the slight physical discomfort from my allergic reaction, all the anxiety around those feelings seemed to melt away. Without knowing it, without having ever learned about it, I had engaged in exposure therapy to rid myself of this obsessive fear. I was able to trust that I was going to be OK, and I was now able to go to sleep and get the much-needed rest I required during finals week.

To my surprise, almost immediately, my anxiety about asphyxiating plummeted.

The OCD Connection

When people have obsessions about the health of their bodies, worry that they might be ill or that they might die, and spend time and energy trying to reassure themselves by going to multiple physicians who tell them that there is nothing to worry about, and/or engage in lengthy research about their presumed medical condition, we diagnose them with hypochondriasis. Some in our profession prefer the term "health anxiety" and see this set of symptoms as distinct from, but very much related to, OCD.

The treatment strategy with this form of OCD is like any other. You label your fear as an excessive reaction, worsen the scenario in your mind on purpose, and prevent yourself from engaging in any reassurance-seeking behavior. You get angry at the fear and challenge it. You "fly into the darkness."

In the memory that I have shared with you in the above story, my reaction to my allergic experience not only was an excessive, phobic reaction to my physical symptoms at the time but was rooted in a very old, almost traumatic experience that I had as a child. If something so old and so ingrained could be turned around so quickly, then it seems reasonable to expect that "flying into the darkness" would be an effective intervention for controlling many OCD symptoms that present as health anxiety.

The Andy Griffith Show

Remember the Andy Griffith Show that was aired during the 1960s? The black-and-white TV fantasy of small-town Middle America was funny and endearing, but mostly, it was comforting. International tensions, drug abuse, the Vietnam War, the generation gap, student riots, and all the other scary and stressful realities of the world at that time did not exist in the little town of Mayberry. For kids of a certain age particularly, the stress of school and other such concerns of a preadolescence slipped away whenever one turned on the TV and entered the world of this quiet little town and the lives of the people who lived there.

For those of you who might be unfamiliar with the characters, or might have just forgotten them, a very brief review: Andy Taylor, played by the singer/actor Andy Griffith, is the town sheriff and a widower who lives with his elderly Aunt Bea, and his young son, Opie (played by Ron Howard who was later to be known as Richie Cunningham of Happy Days fame, and later still to become one of the top movie directors in Hollywood). Opie, Andy, and Aunt Bea make up a kind, warm, and friendly family, and any stresses among them tended to be relatively minor, amusing, and short lived. Their lifestyles exemplified the values of charity, community, and godliness, and, of course, the American way. Although there were other central characters in the TV series (most notably Deputy Barney Fife, played by Don Knotts), the main storyline in any one particular episode revolved around the three characters mentioned. The details of this story might not exactly mirror the original broadcast, but the main theme of the episode is our focus here.

A drifter into town, an older man with a gentle and charismatic personality, has somehow come to the attention of Aunt Bea (the details of how she meets him are nonessential). This visitor was played by Edgar Buchanan who, for you TV Land aficionados, or those old enough to remember, later played the role of Uncle Joe in another black-and-white TV family comedy, Petticoat Junction. Back to our story in Mayberry, Aunt Bea is charmed by this gentleman, as he makes small talk with her and politely compliments her about such things as her beauty and femininity. He seems pleasant enough, and so when he asks Aunt Bea if he could stay in the guest room of her home in exchange for mending and painting her fence, she checks with Andy, and they all agree to this barter arrangement.

As it turns out, the fence gets mended and painted, but not by the visiting gentleman. Instead, the man convinces Opie that he is suffering with some back difficulties and ends up enlisting Opie to do the work for him. He then offers Aunt Bea a further arrangement to continue to stay on as a guest in exchange for painting the porch. Over the next couple of days he takes Aunt Bea out for a picnic (which she cooks and prepares), takes her to the movies (which she actually pays for), goes for walks with her, and plays cards with her. She is enjoying herself, but the porch remains unpainted.

This continues day after day for a couple of weeks. Each time, the visitor promises to complete a project in exchange for room and board, and each time, either someone else ends up doing the project for him, or it remains undone because he is too busy engaged in social activities with Aunt Bea. All the while, he has Aunt Bea doing his laundry, cleaning his room, and washing his dishes, as he sleeps late in the morning, takes afternoon naps in the living room so that everyone has to keep quiet, and eats up all of Andy's favorite Aunt Bea pies for his midnight snacks.

After two weeks, Andy has had enough. At first, Aunt Bea insists that Andy is overreacting, and that the visitor is sincere and honest and will be moving on within the next couple of days. When this does not happen, she again makes excuses for the man, saying that since his back had "gone out" on him earlier that day they could not insist that he leave in such a poor condition. The TV audience is witness to the man's staging this back attack in such a way so that poor Aunt Bea would witness his feigned injury and thus feel guilty kicking him out of the house.

With the visitor still living in the Taylor's house several days later, Aunt Bea finally gives in to Andy. Even though she is still smitten with the man, she begrudgingly admits that things have gotten out of hand,

and she gives permission for Andy to confront the visitor. The episode ends with the man leaving town, followed by news which comes to Andy via his police connections that this visiting gentleman has played out a similar scenario with several unsuspecting and vulnerable older women in other towns and in other counties.

The epilogue scene, which was often used in the series, was one in which Andy has one of his "father and son" talks with Opie. He explains to little Opie the importance of balancing hospitality to strangers with the need for setting boundaries and using a little common sense when it comes to dealing with people who might take advantage of one's kindness. He emphasizes in this heart to heart talk the necessity to be careful not to make someone too comfortable in your home if you want him to leave.

Be careful not to make someone too comfortable in your home if you want him to leave.

The OCD Connection

Don't make someone too comfortable in your home if you want him to leave. This is the lesson that is often lacking in families who deal with OCD when it afflicts one of their own family members. In their attempts to honor the wishes of the family member with OCD, in an effort to reduce his anxiety and to "help" him, well-meaning family members will engage in OCD rituals on behalf of that family member. Parents will say certain words at bedtime in response to the demands of their OCD-afflicted children who say that they cannot go to sleep until those words are spoken. Wives will wash what they know is already clean, husbands will check what they know has already been checked. In so doing, all these family members become extensions of the OCD cycle. They, too, are now caught in the web of thought and activity with no evident means of escape. They have in fact aided and abetted, not the family member, but the OCD itself, making it stronger by giving in to its demands. Rather than challenging it, rather than setting limits with it, they have welcomed it, and they have made it comfortable in their home, and so it stays, it digs its heels in, and it sets roots in their family as it exercises control over everyone.

Like the kindly gentleman on The Andy Griffith Show, OCD knows no boundaries when it comes to hospitality. It knows only to seek out opportunities and exploit them for its own survival. Family members need to learn how to properly challenge the OCD in their home by setting limits with the OCD-afflicted member. In so doing, they help to reduce the influence of the disorder on family life and, in the long run, are doing the best thing that can be done to help not only themselves, but also the person who has the OCD. It is the first step in opening up the front door (or the back one) and showing OCD the way out.

10

In Defense of ERP as an OCD Treatment

Exposure and response prevention (ERP), as a behavioral intervention for the treatment of OCD, has often been criticized and misunderstood by therapists with other psychological orientations. It is sometimes described as being mechanistic and artificial in nature. Critics claim that the relationship between therapist and client can be stilted and distant. They claim that directly treating the symptoms of OCD is misguided and that the underlying causes or needs that are being gratified by these symptoms remain unaddressed.

This chapter is a rebuttal—a presentation, not only of the legitimacy of ERP as an effective way of treating OCD symptoms, but as an explanation of how ERP can serve as a medium by which is forged a strong belief in one's own self-efficacy and also a trust in one's own therapist. These two central building blocks, belief in oneself and trust in one's therapist, are necessary for successful therapy of the more dynamic issues, which, although separate from the OCD itself, often exacerbate or help to define the OCD symptom picture.

Exposure Therapy as a Metaphor

In my practice we see many clients with OCD who come to us after having seen one or more psychodynamic therapists, sometimes over a period of many years. These clients come in frustrated and desperate, having found that their OCD symptoms have persisted despite therapeutic intervention. However, early in their treatment with us, as they begin to learn about and then utilize ERP and begin to experience within a relatively short period of time a significant amelioration of symptoms, they complain that their previous therapists never even mentioned ERP as an alternative intervention. They will often become angry and even appalled that their previous therapists seemed to have had no specific plan or protocol to address their OCD, at least a plan that they were made aware of, and that indeed these symptoms were never even addressed directly.

I personally have known several colleagues who treat OCD from a psychodynamic point of reference, and although the ones with whom I have had in-depth discussions about the treatment of OCD have not held the belief that OCD is the result of improper toilet training (as was commonly thought among many therapists decades ago), they still see OCD primarily as a symbolic representation of unresolved, often unconscious conflicts. This results in a treatment that focuses not on the reduction and control of OC symptoms directly but rather on developing insight and understanding of what these unconscious conflicts might be and working them through to some kind of resolution, with the expectation that once this has been done successfully, the patient will no longer require the OC symptoms as a defense or distraction and will abandon these symptoms.

As a cognitive-behavioral psychologist, I of course differ in my approach, but there are often times when I must admit that a client presents with a clinical picture wherein I can see the temptation to interpret the OC symptoms that are present from a more psychodynamic perspective. Such was the case with a client whom I shall call Larry.

Larry was a 30-something, single, unemployed young man who lived with relatives. His OC symptoms were severe and varied, but the most prominent involved fear of contamination and compulsive washing. I visited him in his home, and in his room he had a drawer full of over 200 single dollar bills that had been washed so thoroughly that the face of President Washington was barely discernible on most of them. His contamination obsessions and resulting anxiety were so debilitating that he had never held a job or had been involved in a dating relationship. He had few friends and was relatively reclusive.

Years before, when Larry lived away at college, he had locked himself out of his car. He phoned his parents, who lived an hour and a half away from campus, and asked his father to drive to the school and bring him the extra set of keys. As his father was driving to the college to deliver the keys to Larry, he was killed in an automobile accident. It was soon after this incident that Larry's symptoms required him to drop out of college, and nothing much had changed in his life over the next decade.

It is easy to see how one can interpret certain OC symptoms as a specific defense against the guilt and pain of a terrible tragedy.

It is easy to see how one can interpret certain OC symptoms as a specific defense against the guilt and pain of a terrible tragedy. Washing, in particular, is often seen as a way of ridding oneself of guilty feelings. Alternatively, one could say that Larry was punishing himself for the death of his father by not allowing himself to move forward in his life or that his focus on the anxiety generated by his OCD symptoms and his attempts to avoid or clean contaminated items served to distract him from the incredibly painful feelings that lie just below the surface of his emotional awareness.

If this was indeed what was happening, then therapy would focus on helping Larry to identify, experience, and share these feelings. This process would take place by the therapist's developing a trusting relationship with Larry in therapy so that he could feel safe enough in the therapeutic relationship to let go of his resistance to addressing these negative feelings. Interventions would include interpretation and reflection. Emotional material might be directed specifically at the therapist through the process known as transference.

Psychodynamic therapists might claim that ERP in such a case essentially misses the point. They might see behavior therapy as a mechanistic, "cookie-cutter" approach to treatment, in which the importance of the therapeutic relationship is secondary to merely teaching these specific skills in order to reduce or eliminate the symptoms. They would claim, and rightly so, that very often reducing the presenting symptoms results in these being replaced by other OC symptoms.

My response to these arguments is that this trauma did not "cause" Larry's OCD. Larry *had* OCD, and the OCD merely capitalized on the trauma once it had occurred. In Larry's case in particular, it was clear through history-taking interviews that Larry's propensity toward OC-like symptoms had predated his father's untimely death. This is often the case when OCD is seen to be the result of a particular life change, life stress, or life trauma. It is as if the OC already exists in some form, at some level, and then, looking around inside asks, "Where can

I cause trouble?" OCD is very opportunistic. It will strike at the Achilles' heel, at every person's weakness, or will take advantage of whatever particular set of circumstances makes itself available.

It is as if the OC already exists in some form, at some level, and then, looking around inside asks, "Where can I cause trouble?"

Many of the OCD-afflicted physicians and nurses whom I have seen in treatment experience a fear that they will make someone sick or make an error with medication resulting in the death of their patients. Accountants present with OC symptoms involving numbers, counting, or orderliness. Grade-school teachers obsess that maybe they are child molesters. People who have grown up in particularly religious households, such as strictly observant Catholics or Orthodox Jews, can present with OC symptoms around what is right or wrong, which we term "scrupulosity." These illustrations all seem to indicate that OCD manifests itself through issues and circumstances that already are part of a person's life. This is an oversimplification and generalization, to be sure, and has no empirical support that I am aware of, but it has been my observation from my own clinical experience and that of the people with whom I have worked over the years.

ERP works. The data clearly indicate that this is the case. But helping Larry touch unwashed dollar bills does not help him better deal with the death of his father. And although ERP might remove some of the obstacles that prevent him from moving forward in his life, it does nothing to better prepare him to do so. This is why, although the cognitive-behavioral treatment of his OCD symptoms is necessary for Larry to rejoin the rest of the human race, it is not sufficient. More is required.

Larry *did* need to talk about his father and that fateful day so many years ago. He also needed to learn the skills that would enable him to reenter the vocational and social worlds from which he was hiding. Both of these challenges required two things. One was a sense of self-efficacy, a heightened self-esteem, and a belief that he could manage the fears that would no doubt be ignited by moving forward in these directions. Second, he needed to fully trust the person who would support and guide him in this process if he was to be successful in not letting his own fears stop him from moving forward.

I propose that nothing under the sun could serve to be a more effective way to help such a person create a sense of self-empowerment, increase his self-esteem and self-efficacy, and learn that he can successfully challenge and transcend his own fears than through the process of ERP directed at one's OCD symptoms. By engaging in ERP work, such a person learns that he can do what he thought could not be done. One learns not to trust the fear, but to trust in one's own capacity to transcend one's fear.

And what could be a more effective way to nurture the trust in a guide than to have that guide support you through the process of ERP? We have all heard the stories of those corporate team-building retreats, where a person confronts fears of walking barefoot through hot coals. By going through such a process one learns not only to expand one's own self-expectations but also learns to more fully trust the person who cried out in the moment of confrontation, "You can do it!"

And so ERP, through its natural process of building self-efficacy and engendering trust in the therapist, becomes the perfect metaphor for those tasks yet to follow—facing the inner emotional pain as yet unexplored and facing the "real life" fears of moving forward in one's life. After the fire walk, the corporate executive feels stronger and more capable to face the challenges of his profession and more readily trusts and feels able to rely on the support of those individuals who rallied behind him as he confronted that fire walk. Likewise ERP, far from missing the point, not only directly addresses the control or even elimination of the OCD symptoms themselves, but allows the client to be better prepared to move forward in addressing the other life issues that remain once the OCD itself has been reigned in.

Conclusions

For Those Who Have OCD, Their Families and Friends, as Well as the Clinicians Who Treat Them

If you have read the stories in this book, you now have a sort of "shorthand" that you can use whenever you think about or talk about OCD.

You understand that the paradoxical treatment of exposure and response prevention involves "flying into the darkness" and that while you have to repeatedly "go to a horror movie" in order to insure your recovery, you can still control at what end and how quickly you "enter into a swimming pool." You know that it can be helpful to see your disorder as the "bully in the playground," that you have to behave as a "predator rather than prey," and that you should challenge your OCD in an unconventional way by "breaking the statue on the mantelpiece." When you become afraid because you tell yourself that treatment will be too hard and you will get overwhelmed, you now can remind yourself about "the best man" and remember not to think the way a child does about "eating Brussels sprouts." When you experience a rebound of your OCD symptoms after challenging them, you know to keep in mind that this is just the "paper tiger" having a "temper tantrum."

Parents need to remember to put on their own oxygen masks first when "preparing for takeoff," and family members need to remember the "Andy Griffith Show" lest they make OCD too comfortable in their home. Hoarders need to remember "Aunt Molly's cookies," whereas those with health anxiety OCD should recall "mushroom pizza." And so it is with all the stories reviewed in this book—each has associated with it a word or a phrase that can become a shorthand in communication.

Old friends who have shared many experiences and memories can often say just a single word or a phrase to each other that makes reference to an event that might have taken place many years before. In a brief instant, that word or phrase can communicate an entire story along with the emotions that the story stimulates. It allows the old friend to share with the person with whom he is talking a deep and personal bond created via a shared history. In a like manner, you and I, and everyone else who has read these stories, now have such a bond. We can speak our own private language, and we know exactly what each other means.

As a person with OCD, when you struggle with challenging your OC fears because they feel so real, and you comment, "I am having trouble remembering that 'there is no spoon,'" you know that I understand in a very personal way. When I remind you that your anticipatory anxiety about facing a fear is just a "white-water rafting" reaction, images and emotions are communicated with my words. Thus, by making references to these stories, you can share with others, and they can support you in a way that will help you feel less isolated and more understood.

As a family member or friend, you now have not only a better insider's viewpoint into the world of OCD, a phenomenological understanding of the inner life of the OCD-afflicted person, but also you have tools that you can use to remind that person that you stand by him. For you and for the professionals who work with this disorder, you can engender a greater level of trust that comes from sharing a personal language, a private memory, a common experience. This elevated sense of trust in the family, friends, and mental health professionals who stand with her serves the purpose of allowing the person with OCD to better remember "Peanuts" and the lesson to *not* trust her OCD fears but rather to trust in herself. Finally, we should expect that this trust ultimately leads to her more easily finding the courage to better "fly into the darkness."

You can engender a greater level of trust that comes from sharing a personal language, a private memory, a common experience.

I hope that these stories have successfully served their purpose of providing a different perspective into the experience of having, living with, and treating OCD. But you need not limit yourself to these sixty-plus stories. Rather, you may view them as prototypes or illustrations of how you can develop and utilize your own stories for the purpose of better understanding and recovering from OCD. The stories in this book may serve as a solid foundation onto which you can build, providing narratives from your own personal experience or imagination.

Some of the stories I have shared with you here were actual experiences from my own past. The personal nature of these stories raises the emotional power behind them and increases the "connectedness" on the part of the listener. What I mean by this is that because you know I am sharing an actual personal experience from my history, you also know that I have experienced the same kinds of thoughts and emotions and engaged in the same kinds of behaviors that you have within the context of your OCD world. This serves to intensify the sense that you are understood, that you are not alone, and that you are not so strangely different from the rest of "us."

I encourage you to create your own stories. Illustrate, illuminate, and clarify *your* OCD experiences through the creation of your own metaphors. Further expand the scope and depth of the collection in this book by adding to it your own narratives that touch on those aspects of the OCD experience that are most salient to you. You will find such an endeavor to be therapeutic and empowering.

And when you have a really good one, consider sending it to me. If you have several really good ones, send them all. I will collect them, hopefully use them to the benefit of my clients and their families, and perhaps organize them and have them published as a follow-up to the present collection. You may be identified as the author, or, if you prefer, remain anonymous. In any event, you will become part of the recovery process for a stranger (or many strangers, for that matter) whom you have never met yet with whom you share a very private life experience.

A final note to those of you who experience OCD firsthand. I find that this line of work forces me to be more honest with myself about facing my own fears (which is why I had to take on that challenge of walking across the glass in the CN Tower). I would hope and expect that the same dynamic would operate for you. By sharing your stories with others who may also have OCD, by helping them to face *their* fears, you may ultimately feel compelled to fully challenge yourself and fly into the darkness at every opportunity.

Appendix: Index of Stories

Additional Resources

Abramowitz, J. (2009). *Getting over OCD: A 10-step workbook for taking back your life*. New York: The Guilford Press.

Baer, L. (2001). *Getting control: Overcoming your obsessions and compulsions* (Rev. ed.). New York: Plume.

Baer, L. (2002). *The imp of the mind. Exploring the silent epidemic of obsessive bad thoughts*. New York: Plume.

Chansky, T E. (2001). *Freeing your child from obsessive-compulsive disorder: A powerful, practical program for parents of children and adolescents*. New York: Three Rivers Press, 2001.

Foa, E. B., Wilson, R. (2001). *Stop obsessing! How to overcome your obsessions and compulsions* (Rev. ed.). New York: Bantam Books.

Grayson, J. (2003). *Freedom from obsessive-compulsive disorder: A personalized recovery program for living with uncertainty*. New York: Tarcher/Penguin Putnam.

Hyman, B. M., Pedrick, C. (2005). *The OCD workbook: Your guide to breaking free from obsessive-compulsive disorder*. Oakland, CA: New Harbinger.

March, J. S., & Mulle, K. (1998). *OCD in children and adolescents: A cognitive behavioral treatment manual*. New York: The Guilford Press.

Neziroglu, F., & Yaryura-Tobias, J. (1997). *Over and over again: Understanding obsessive-compulsive disorder* (Updated and Rev. ed.). Hoboken, NJ: Jossey-Bass.

Osborn, I. (1999). *Tormenting thoughts and secret rituals: The hidden epidemic of obsessive-compulsive disorder*. New York: Dell Publishing Company.

Penzel, F. (2000). *Obsessive-compulsive disorders: A complete guide to getting well and staying well*. New York: Oxford University Press.

Rapoport, J. L. (1997). *The boy who couldn't stop washing: The experience and treatment of obsessive-compulsive disorder.* New York: Signet Books.

Steketee, G., & White, K. (1990). *When once is not enough: Help for obsessive compulsives.* Oakland, CA: New Harbinger Publications.

Van Noppen, B. L., Tortora Pato, M., & Rasmussen, S. (1997). *Learning to live with OCD: Obsessive compulsive disorder* (4th ed.). Milford, CT: Obsessive Compulsive Foundation.

Weg, A. H. (2009). Storytelling and the use of metaphor with OCD. In Roberts, A. R. (Ed.), *Social workers' desk reference* (2nd Ed). New York: Oxford University Press, 2009.